DREAM
DICTIONARY

DREAM
DICTIONARY

EVERYTHING YOU NEED TO KNOW
TO INTERPRET YOUR DREAMS AND
MAKE THEM WORK FOR YOU

COMPREHENSIVE EXPLANATIONS
OF SYMBOLS, ARCHETYPES, AND
INTERPRETATIONS

Antonia Beattie

THUNDER BAY
P · R · E · S · S
SAN DIEGO, CALIFORNIA

*There seems to be
something in dream images . . .
we have the feeling they might
mean something.*

—SAMUEL TAYLOR COLERIDGE

CONTENTS

INTRODUCTION

The Interpretation and Power of Dreams

Our normal waking consciousness is but one special type of consciousness, while all about it parted by the filmiest of screens there lie potential forms of consciousness entirely different.

—William James

Have you ever had the pleasure of being able to fly around your home, or found yourself talking to Auntie Mabel—who has been dead for years—or seen yourself in the mirror looking younger and without the customary set of wrinkles?

Such activities would be unheard of in our daily life, but in dreams anything is possible. We all dream. We dream every night, whether we remember it or not. We live in two worlds: the "real world," when we are conscious and awake, and the "illusionary world," when we are asleep. Dreaming comes spontaneously to us all. It is one of our greatest powers.

Our dreams can affect us intensely. They can move us by their emotional and spiritual force so that we awaken in tears or excited by an experience or an idea. We may have sensory experiences while we dream, feeling, hearing, smelling and tasting, as well as seeing visual imagery. We may even imagine, as we lie half-awake, that the vivid dream experience we have just had was real.

Dreams are one of the most powerful means we have of communicating with ourselves. They can allow us to understand ourselves. They act as a metaphor or story that reveals to us our desires, our longings, and our secrets.

They also show us our fears and limitations. They allow us to sort out our challenges and work out our issues. They send us the message that some aspects of our lives are unresolved, or give us guidance about future events or issues.

One of the mind's primary jobs is to maintain the data that it has collected during the day. When we are asleep the mind processes this information, discarding the pieces that are not relevant or needed. The dream state is where we do most of this work.

Dream messages come through the subconscious mind, which is the storehouse of our emotions, habits, and behaviors. This part of our mind communicates with the self via symbols and images. It is important that we understand these symbols and images so that we can work out what our dreams mean, what messages they are sending us.

Our dreams often present us with images and sequences that seem random, but these images were specially chosen by our higher, conscious mind, which is the source of our knowingness, intuition, and openness to a higher awareness.

Although your dream memories may be foggy and fragmented at the moment, you can learn some techniques for deciphering the messages of your dreams. But first you need to prepare yourself so that you are able to recall and record the dreams you generate (see pages 8–15). The second stage is to understand what your dreams mean. This involves developing an awareness of symbols and of your responses to these symbols. This can help you control your waking world using the messages received from your dreams.

To understand your dreams and learn how to build your own personal symbol dictionary, see pages 16–23. A full dream symbols dictionary can be found on pages 24–163. Different techniques on how to work with your dreams, such as communicating with your dream self, and how to effectively tap into the power of your dreams, are discussed on pages 164–187.

DREAM TIP
Your sleep and dreams

When you wake refreshed and clearheaded, chances are that during your dream state you have examined an aspect of your life and have clarified it. Feeling confused upon waking may be a signal that the issue is still relevant and you are not sure how to deal with it. The subconscious will then use different dreams to give you further opportunities to resolve the matter.

The First Steps

> *Swift as a shadow, short as any dream.*
> —William Shakespeare, *A Midsummer Night's Dream*, act 1, scene 1

We spend a third of our lives sleeping, and we dream while we are doing so. In a lifetime, by conservative estimates, six to seven years are spent dreaming. It is important to prepare ourselves to capture these dreams and make the most of them. Sometimes we go through phases where our dreams are scary and we would rather not focus on the images our mind generates. However, there are a number of things we can do in our waking life that will have a positive impact on our dreams.

If you suffer from negative dreams, you will find that if you can deal with situations, fears, and problems in your waking life you will actually release the need to bring out the problem in the dream state. You may do this through active conscious thought, positive affirmations, or meditations (see pages 14–15). Meditation can prepare you for a good night's sleep and for the dream state. You might like to try a simple meditation in a quiet place before going to bed—perhaps in a bath full of warm, scented water, with the bathroom lit by a single candle. Whether or not you successfully deal with the issue, some of the experiences will still be relived during sleep, but they will have a far less negative impact. Many people find listening to music an effective way to induce a sense of tranquillity before entering the dream state—try instrumental, classical (particularly baroque), or ambient recordings (such as Brian Eno).

There are many breathing techniques to relax you in preparation for either meditation or sleep. You might like to try this one: Clear your mind, and slowly count to four. Inhale deeply through your nose and take the air deep into your abdomen. Hold it for a moment. Again to a count of four, very slowly exhale through your mouth and, as you exhale, feel yourself letting go of all your stress and tension.

Feel every muscle in your body becoming soft and loose and comfortable. Take a few moments, as you relax completely, for a mental tour of your body. Take time to notice anywhere you still feel any tension or stress and let it go. Repeat this process for a minimum of three inhalations and three exhalations. Become aware of how much more you relax mentally and physically with each breath you let go. For maximum benefit, keep repeating these steps for one to three minutes.

To help you to remember your dreams, just before you go to sleep, breathe deeply and focus mentally. Say to yourself that you wish to remember clearly any dream you have. If you keep making this affirmation, you will soon find it easier to remember your dreams.

The contents of a dream can vanish in minutes unless you record them in some way immediately, so if you wake from a dream during the night, record it at once. Don't be tempted to wait until morning. As soon as you wake, mentally replay the main points of your dream about three times, capturing more detail with each replay. Next, record each dream on a separate piece of paper or via a small tape recorder kept at your bedside. See pages 10–11 on how to set up a dream journal.

DREAM TIP
Dealing with frightening dreams

Sometimes a frightening dream seems so real that you might fear the events actually happening in your waking life. Remember that dreams are symbolic. A frightening dream is only trying to show you that you are fearful of something in your life that you are not confronting or resolving. Your protective subconscious is trying to help you achieve clarity so that you can grow.

Setting Up a Dream Journal

Something we were withholding made us weak,
until we found it was ourselves.

—Robert Frost

Dreaming occurs when we are asleep and our mind shows black and white or colored pictures, moving or still, that relate to our life. When we dream we are organizing and archiving memories and experiences. Our thoughts are moving naturally between the conscious, subconscious, and higher conscious minds, creating dreams.

Research has shown that dreams can have meaning. Our dreams are multilayered messages from within, stemming from our deeper unconscious. They can help us in our emotional, psychological, and spiritual evolution and growth. Philosophies about dreaming are many, but they have a common focus: we communicate with ourselves through our dreams. Our higher conscious mind and our subconscious mind bring data to the attention of our conscious self.

The first step toward interpreting your dreams is starting a dream journal. This is the best way to remember and record your dreams. Your unconscious mind uses dream signs and symbols (see "Dream symbols," on pages 24–163). After at least ten nights of dreaming (not necessarily consecutive), you will notice these symbols recurring. This will give you ample material for learning your own dream language. As you analyze and study your dreams, you will discover their central themes. Here is a seven-step strategy for using your dream journal.

1 Give yourself a reminder as you are drifting off to sleep that you wish to remember your dreams. Keep reminding yourself about this. Eventually it will work, and your dreams will be vivid as you awake.

2 Upon waking, immediately begin recording your dream in your dream journal.

3 Date and title your dream when you begin recording it.

4 Write your dream in the present tense—this will help return you

to the state and experience of the dream, and you will remember more details.

5 Make a note of the emotions you felt in the dream, and its overall tone. Were you fearful or courageous, happy or sad?

6 Jot down the significant events and feelings in your life at the moment—this will offer clues to what your dream was about.

7 Go back mentally through your dream. List each possible symbol and theme. Ask your conscious thinking mind what the symbols mean; then ask your subconscious mind what the message is.

PERSONAL DREAM JOURNAL
Sample entry

Date: Title of dream:

Time went to sleep: Time awoke:

Location of dream:

DREAM:

My role: Active/Passive/Observer/Participant

Key characters:

Period, landscape, environment:

Feelings and emotions during dream:

Significant events and feelings in my life at the moment:

SYMBOLS:

* Dream symbol:

* Conscious symbol:

* Message:

Don't forget to record these symbols in your personal symbol dictionary (see pages 22–23)

Summary (conclusions about my dream, messages it's giving me, and how I should act on this):

Using Dream Crystals

We are such stuff
As dreams are made on; and our little life
Is rounded with a sleep.

—William Shakespeare, *The Tempest*, act 4, scene I

For some, dreaming haphazardly is not good enough. Our forefathers, and shamans of both distant ages and today, used crystals and other dream enhancers to enrich their dreams. Crystals are natural, perfect amplifiers and transformers that will influence your physical, emotional, and mental energies when you are awake and when you are asleep. They can help you create abundance and happiness in your life, promote good health and good relationships, and more. When selecting a crystal, choose one that you are drawn to. If your crystal is not described in this book, find out its purpose and utilize it in the way that best supports you. Keep your crystals

NAME	COLOR	FUNCTION
Amber	Golden/honey	Regenerates, increases energy levels.
Amethyst	Purple	Promotes healing, natural harmony and well-being.
Citrine	Yellow/orange	Revitalizes the body, releases stress, tension and pain.
Clear quartz	White, clear, mostly transparent	Gives clarity, draws out the negative, stores and amplifies feelings.
Diamond	Clear	Gives focus, direction.
Lapis lazuli	Dark blue	Heals the emotions, gives courage and strength.
Peridot	Light green	Releases negative programming.
Pyrite	Gold	Clears frustration and traumas, balances awareness.
Rose quartz	Pink	The love stone; creates and enhances love and harmony.
Ruby	Red	Promotes the healing of heart matters and maintains balance in the body.
Tiger's eye	Black and yellow	Protects, grounds.
Turquoise	Turquoise	Protects, opens throat chakra, guards against adversaries.

clear and clean by putting them outside on a moonlit night and then washing them in salt water (do not use detergents). Anoint your crystal with a scented oil—one that has pleasant, calming associations for you. See the list opposite for some of the more common dream crystals.

For dream work, it is best to keep your crystal beside your bed or under your pillow. You could even hold it in your hand during sleep or meditation. For best results, use the following technique.

CRYSTAL DREAMING TECHNIQUE

1 Choose a crystal that relates to the concern or challenge you wish to work on.

2 Go to the place where you normally sleep or a place where you meditate. Make sure you feel safe and comfortable there and are not going to be disturbed.

3 Hold the crystal in your hand or place it near you.

4 With your eyes closed, go within, and center yourself by focusing on a point that is, in your mind's eye, in front of you and above eye level.

5 Expand your awareness to encompass the whole of yourself, from the top of your head to the tips of your toes. Imagine a bubble or cocoon all around you.

6 Ask for help with whatever your concern or challenge may be.

7 Holding the stone or concentrating upon it, and taking deep breaths in, imagine getting clarity and balance as you drop the question into the stone.

8 Let the question go, and allow yourself to begin floating back down to your awake state (if you wish to return), or deeper into your dream-time sleep.

9 When you return to the waking state you will be refreshed and unconcerned about the outcome, knowing things are working out.

10 Record your dream, including any images and symbols.

11 Now ask yourself how you feel about the concern or challenge you had. See if you feel differently about it, and make a note of any insights.

A Meditation for Remembering Dreams

To sleep, perchance to dream.

—William Shakespeare, *Hamlet*, act 2, scene 1

We are just beginning to understand the special gifts that dreaming gives us. Our dreams help us to find outlets for expression and often contain clues about important needs. For instance, if our dreams frighten us, we may have a worry that our conscious mind is repressing. If our dreams are puzzling, we may need to get more information. Vivid, recurring, or serial dreams may be dreams that have special messages for us.

However, if you have difficulty remembering the images of your dreamscape—and your feelings while you are dreaming—try the following simple meditation to help you remember your dreams. First, find a quiet, comfortable place where you will not be disturbed. Then read the following instructions into a tape recorder. You may then wish to record some ambient or classical music onto your tape—this will help you fall asleep feeling peaceful and calm.

Read the instructions slowly and calmly, perhaps with a bit of a lilt in your voice. Take your time, visualizing how you would feel at each stage of the instructions.

Play the tape just before you go to sleep or when you are doing your meditation during the day. When you are meditating, the instructions will help bring your dreams to your conscious mind. When you sleep and dream, they will help you remember your dreams.

REMEMBERING YOUR DREAMS
Meditation instructions

1 Lie comfortably on your bed with your legs and arms uncrossed. Feel the bed sheets around your body and know that you are safe and warm.

2 Close your eyes and experience the feeling of relaxation. Allow your thoughts about everyday concerns to melt away. Become aware of a wave of relaxation pouring over you, starting at your toes and ending at the top of your head. You will start feeling

---

that you are drifting deeper and deeper into a state of relaxation and happiness.

3 Become aware of the images that are coming to you while you are feeling relaxed. Let yourself follow the flow of images that come as you drift deeper. Do not be concerned that as soon as you notice any image, thought, or form, it changes.

4 Allow the images to flow in and out. Notice that you can choose to have any kind of thought you wish.

5 You can choose to go beyond "normal" dreams. You can choose to fly, to see an old friend, to get answers to problems, to find peace and harmony.

6 Now relax, and breathe slowly and deeply.

7 Imagine that you are drifting, going deeper and deeper; your conscious mind is becoming passive, allowing your subconscious mind to take control.

8 Expand your awareness to encompass yourself, the room, the place where you are sitting, the building, the block, the city, the state, and so on. Let this awareness expand and grow.

9 Connect to this awareness, and let a symbol, a gift from within, form and come into your space, your imagination, your inner vision.

10 Breathe, and feel the peace, tranquillity, harmony, balance and oneness. Accept the gift.

11 Note how you feel about this gift, this space and place.

12 Start to come back. Do it slowly and easily. Become aware of the here and now. Open your eyes and wiggle your toes to ground yourself, and return to your conscious mind.

[If you are doing this tape to send yourself to sleep, omit this last instruction.]

UNDERSTANDING YOUR DREAMS

Deciphering the Messages

We must inquire what dreams are, and from what cause sleepers sometimes dream and sometimes do not, or whether the truth is that sleepers always dream but don't always remember; and if this occurs, what its explanation is.

—Aristotle

Using our dreams means using the guiding principle that is buried deep within us. Learning the forgotten language of our inner world is the true means of empowering our lives. Dream language is a truly universal language that can be understood and learned by people of all ages, cultures, and levels of education. Knowing the language of our dreams helps us open new pathways into our minds, strengthen our awareness, and liberate ourselves, as we realize that we are multidimensional beings.

Dreams have their own unique meanings. The knowledge of these meanings can give us a real understanding of what we dream about, and of our lives as a whole. It is important that we devote some time and patience to learning to understand our dreamscapes and the messages that are being sent to us via our subconscious and higher conscious minds. In the process, we can learn a new language—the language of our dreams.

Each dream is of a specific type, and contains themes and symbols that can tell us about our nature, our preoccupations and our innermost needs. The person in the dream is present in a story or a scene and the dreamer is either the subject of the dream or plays the spectator. Dreams being what they are, the perspective of the dream can shift between the dreamer being a participant and a spectator. Dreams can also be multisensory experiences, where we can revel in the sensation of touch, smell, sight, taste, and hearing.

However, the dreamer may be able to understand some conversations without any actual words being spoken. Each person has his or her own vocabulary of dreams. Noting recurring themes can help you build up your own language of dreams. There are some common philosophies on the nature and value of dreaming, including that dreaming:

- consolidates what we have learned from the events of the day;
- provides a workshop for self-repair and competency;
- provides information to help the dreamer with decisions;
- highlights the imbalances and unrealized potentials in our lives, and brings them to our conscious attention so that we can seek improvement;
- encourages us to reach for our desires;
- connects us with the guidance of our higher conscious minds;
- helps achieve harmony among body, mind, and spirit; and
- rids us of the needless thoughts, accumulated during our conscious (awake) hours, that have no significance in our lives.

DREAM HISTORY
Dream research in the 1940s and 1950s

In the late 1940s and early 1950s, research laboratories were established at universities and hospitals around the world to learn more about dreaming. Psychologists or psychiatrists usually supervised these activities, observing—and often controlling equipment—from outside cubicles. In the cubicles, sleepers would be hooked up to an EEG (electroencephalograph), an instrument that monitors brain waves, breathing, and body movements. Observers would awaken sleepers at certain times and ask if they were dreaming. This led to the discovery that there were links between eye movement, brain waves, and dreaming. This was a giant breakthrough in dream research. People reported remembering more dreams when they were in dream laboratories than they did in their normal sleeping environments.

This is where the theory of conscious (creative) dreaming first arose. According to this theory, if the mind is aware of the intention to dream and remember, then it will often do so.

Dream Analysis in Five Easy Steps

*All the things one has forgotten
scream for help in dreams.*

—Elias Canetti, *The Human Province*

Through understanding the language of our dreams, we can reach an understanding of ourselves. Working with our dreams and interpreting their symbols will take time, but this will be time well spent helping ourselves grow. Here are five steps for dream analysis.

1 Recall and record the dream (see pages 10–11, 164–165).
2 Define the type of dream: whether it was a nightmare or a dream you often experience, for example (see pages 168–169).
3 Note whether the dream focused on the past, present, or future.
4 Note your feelings and emotions upon waking.
5 Note the specific symbols belonging to each dream and their associations for you (see pages 170–173).

When you start a journal of your dreams, it is important to keep a journal (of some sort) of your waking life, too. If you compare this with your dreams, you should be able to see how the two fit together and find the key to unlocking your personal symbolism. Use your gut feelings and the information contained in this book in your analysis. Using this process, you should gain greater insight into yourself, your limitations, and your concerns.

An alphabetical index of the symbols in your dreams could also be very useful. Without thinking about the dream itself, simply list the symbols or dream images or items you can remember from it. Then list all the ideas and feelings that you associate with them. Remember, there can be more than one meaning to a symbol. Just as our ideas change, personal symbolic meanings can also change. Soon you should be able to determine what your own dream symbols mean to you as an individual (see pages 22–23 for how to build your own personal symbol dictionary).

Many symbols have several meanings, and these meanings might seem to be incompatible with each other and with their personal meaning for you. Correct interpretation involves assessing the symbol within the context of the dream or series of dreams and with reference to your own life. However, it is generally true to say that happiness in your physical, waking state is always represented by something beautiful in your dreams, and that fear and anxiety in your life is always represented by an unpleasant dream image.

DREAM FACT
REM and NREM

In 1953 it was discovered that when a sleeper is experiencing rapid eye movement (REM), he or she is dreaming. During REM, blood pressure and heart rate increase. The mind is active, but the body has little to no movement (though some people's facial muscles and limbs will move).

For nearly one-third of our lives we are dreaming, and most of that time is spent in REM. REM sleep occurs several times during the sleep cycle. Most people have three to five REM sleeps per night.

There are also periods of non-rapid eye movement (NREM) during sleep. These occur when the sleeper is in a deep sleep. Although dreams occur in both REM and NREM, the NREM dreams seem to have no mental content.

The body requires both REM and NREM sleep.

A normal person spends about 25 percent of her sleeping time in REM. Many factors can interfere with REM sleep, such as drugs (including prescribed sedatives and sleeping pills), alcohol, caffeine, depression, and psychological disorders.

In the early 1960s, dream researchers found that sleep and REM deprivation lead to fatigue, poor concentration, irritability, and memory loss. Total sleep deprivation causes illness and mental disorders.

Recent research has shown that people suffering from serious depression dream less often than the average. As depression sufferers start getting well they begin having more REM dreams.

Six Common Types of Dreams

The treasured dreams of times long past.

—William Wordsworth

Dreams communicate to us in different kinds of ways, depending on their type. Uncovering the meaning of your dream symbols may seem a complicated task at first, but the rewards will be immense. Stick to a routine to make sure you practice regularly, so that your interpretation skills improve. Once you become adept, you can use your dreams to work out the challenges that face you and to predict what could happen in your future. Most of your dreams will probably fit into one of the following categories.

1 **Cleaning-the-mind dreams** are dreams that sort through the emotional and mental clutter caused by whatever has been on your conscious and subconscious minds. Having a cleaning dream is like having the trash collector take away the trash. Think how much junk and clutter we accumulate—we input an immense amount into our minds every day, from television, radio, the Internet, newspapers, and numerous sounds and scenes in the background.

2 **Challenge-conquering and problem-solving dreams** are dreams that can help you tap into information and understand valuable messages. Sometimes you may feel utterly exhausted after dreams of this type.

3 **Teaching dreams** are those that let you make discoveries and receive inspiration on how to handle a person or a situation, usually in your current life. They come from the higher conscious mind and can be very valuable in your waking life.

4 **Premonition or intuition dreams** often give you some kind of foreknowledge—a peek at something that will happen in the future. These dreams have a special feeling about them.

5 **Visionary and prophetic dreams** come from the higher conscious mind, which is connected to the soul. These dreams frequently come with insights, realizations, and a sense of knowingness. They often come to help make sense of spiritual matters in our lives.

6 **Environmental dreams** are produced when something in the environment is integrated into the dream story—a phone ringing, a song playing on a radio, a hot room, a meowing cat, barking dogs, or a vehicle starting up. A full bladder or physical illness can also infiltrate your dreams.

Sometimes our dreams don't fit one of the above types, but are only dream fragments. However, even fragments are important to record, because they act as a summary, containing the essence of a dream. For common dream themes, see pages 168–169.

DREAM HISTORY
The ancient Greeks

The ancient Greeks gave the name oneiromancy to the interpretation of dreams (from the words *oneiros*, meaning dream, and *manteia*, meaning divination). They believed the dreamer was in contact with the gods. In later centuries, Hippocrates, Aristotle, and Galen professed that dreams often contained physiological information that heralded future illnesses. Greek healers taught that colored—as distinct from black and white—dreams balanced thought with feelings, and would enable the body to recover while asleep and become well equipped to deal with life.

Building Your Personal Symbol Dictionary

*I've dreamt in my life dreams that have
stayed with me ever after, and changed my ideas;
they've gone through and through me, like wine
through water, and altered the colour of my mind.*

—Emily Jane Brontë

Our dreams speak to us in symbols: objects, stories, and pictures. Symbols are the way we communicate with our inner selves, a type of personal shorthand, far easier to interpret than verbal communication. Once we know our own symbols, we always get the message. As you record your dreams in your dream journal (see pages 10–11) and examine them for symbols, themes, aspects, and archetypes (see pages 170–173), you can also record their meanings in your personal symbol dictionary (see the example below). Keep this separately from your dream journal (see a sample opposite). Over time, you will discover that your personal symbols bear similar meanings in all your dreams.

PERSONAL SYMBOL DICTIONARY: SAMPLE ENTRY
Date:

Dream Description:

DREAM SYMBOL	CONSCIOUS SYMBOL	MESSAGE
Party	Fun, people, activity	I'm trying to have fun, be happy
Food	Nourishment	I need knowledge
Unfamiliar people	Loneliness, no one knows me	I don't know myself
Dip	Flavor added	I need to add zest to my life
Two blind people	Two wise people	Positive message from both the masculine and the feminine aspects of the self
Clasping hands	Something joined together	The need to blend mind and heart
Rising up	Ascending	Going above for clarity

To complete an entry in your dictionary, do the following.

1 In column 1, write down the symbol from your dream.

2 In column 2, write your answer to the question, "What does this symbol mean to me?" Allow yourself to move outside the context of the dream and within yourself to discover its meaning. For instance, a snake may mean creepiness, threat, or poison in your life, but it could also reflect wisdom and adaptability.

3 In column 3, expand your awareness as you go within and look for message this symbol is giving you. Ask yourself, "What is the message from this symbol?"

When you are completing the entry, try to keep your mind quiet and relaxed. You may wish to become one of the characters or symbols, or ask a symbol what it is trying to tell you. If you come upon a dream image you can't figure out, just let it sit in your mind. The message will eventually be revealed, as inner guidance will always prevail.

DREAM SYMBOL INTERPRETATION: SAMPLE ENTRY

Dream theme: Being chased by a bull

Dream description: I'm in a field with a few people, none I can remember, yet we are friendly. I notice a bull in another field close by, and yet I am not concerned. Suddenly the bull is in my field and chasing me. I'm running and jumping fences and the bull is doing the same. No matter where I go it follows. All of a sudden I decide to jump up on a house. Then the bull just disappears.

My role: Active/Participant

Key characters: A few other people and the bull.

Period, landscape, environment: Time frame is now, landscape is an open field, dream is in color, lots of fences.

Symbols: Bull, fences, chasing, house

Feelings and emotions during dream: Fear, frustration, relief, clarity

DREAM SYMBOL	CONSCIOUS SYMBOL	MESSAGE
Bull—may be archetypal, Anima and Animus	Strength, danger	There's something solid I'm not facing, maybe a barrier, maybe emotions, inner potential
Fences	Boundaries	What seem to be obstacles in life
House	Structure in life	Safe haven
Chasing	Running away	I'm not facing something
Jumping up	Rising above trouble	Clarity is gained when I rise above problems

ABUNDANCE

Feelings of abundance in a dream usually signal a growth in your creativity and your insights, and the rewards flowing from such an increase. This is an indication that you may feel free to accept and enjoy the fruits of your labors.

If you see yourself enjoying a particular type of abundance (for example, if you are surrounded by towers of coins), this may well mean that you should start conserving your resources and finding alternative ways of making a living. Review your work situation and your finances.

However, if you see yourself surrounded by a variety of abundance, and you feel fulfilled by your wealth, you will find that you will be lucky in your ventures. After this kind of dream, make sure to keep your eyes open for any opportunities that will further your goals.

ABYSSES

When you see yourself standing near an abyss, you are most probably facing an important obstacle in your life, particularly in your love life (if the abyss has water at the bottom) or your finances (if the abyss is dry). Be very careful how you treat these matters in your waking hours. If, in your dream, you walk away from the abyss, this may indicate that you are not tackling the issue; if you fall in, it may suggest that you are likely to experience some losses and misunderstandings. If you dream that you somehow step or fly over the abyss and make it to the other side, you have the ability and the opportunity to overcome your problems.

ACCIDENTS

SEE ALSO **MEDICAL MATTERS**, PAGE 103.

Dreaming of an accident is generally a warning that you may suffer some reversals in terms of your finances or love life. Be very careful if you are making long-term arrangements around this time. If you dreamed that you suffered an accident while driving your car, be careful the next day to take extra precautions while driving. Some experts even suggest avoiding driving the car and taking the bus or train to work for the next day or so.

Use your intuition to help you decide whether your dream is prophetic, or is letting you know that you may be "tripped up" in some way if you continue on your current course of action.

Your accident dreams may be accompanied by dreams of you being in pain or injured in a particular part of your body. Experiencing pain in a dream is a common symbol of a need to release deep-seated emotions in a situation where you fear being judged by others.

A dream of injury to the lower part of your body generally represents self-harm; to the upper part, harm inflicted upon you by others. A dreamed experience of injury or bruising to the stomach usually signifies that someone you care about has—or will—hurt you. An eye injury suggests that you are not facing facts.

Dreams of a broken arm or leg often reflect a fear of failure, of being unable to complete tasks set by others or to match their expectations, and feelings of helplessness. A dream of cut or bleeding hands might be symptomatic of feeling worn out and drained of energy.

Burnt fingers indicate a fear of mistakes, of incompetence or of starting a task ill prepared. If a hand is missing fingers, the dream could be expressing guilt and fear of retribution. A dream in which you have skinned knees usually indicates that you are suffering from hurt feelings and want a little extra tender loving care. It also often reflects your need to give more support to your inner child, especially when your vulnerability is being exposed.

AIRCRAFT

SEE ALSO **TRAVEL**, PAGE 146.

Dreaming of aircraft travel usually suggests that you are looking forward to a trip. The symbols of flying and movement, however, represent personal growth, intellectual and creative expansion, and new awareness through fresh stimuli. Dreaming about traveling on an airplane is also often an omen that you will soon receive news about a relative overseas.

Images of an aircraft taking off might indicate that you are preparing to launch into a new area. If you dream that you are excited by the take-off, you will find that you will greatly enjoy your new project. If you feel frightened, there may well be something that you have forgotten or overlooked in your preparations for your new venture.

If you dream that the aircraft is landing, this can signal the conclusion of a job or relationship. An aircraft that makes a smooth landing might reflect your conscious awareness that an aspect of your life is coming to an end, and that everything will work out. If, however, it is a crash landing, then you are not comfortable with the "ending."

A dream of an air crash may also mean that you feel out of control and unsure of what you should do next. If you dream that you experience great turbulence while in the air, it might be a warning of uncertainties ahead of you.

If you dream that you are piloting an airplane, you will find that unexpected acknowledgment or reward will come your way in the near future. The airplane in this situation can symbolize a large project that you will skillfully navigate and execute.

If you dream that you have been traveling by air for a lengthy period, and particularly if this is a recurring dream, you may find that your head is ruling your heart in your love relationship—you will need to rebalance the situation.

ALIENS AND OTHERWORLDLY ENTITIES

Dreams of aliens usually indicate awareness of matters beyond comprehension or a failure to understand another's point of view about you. If you meet an alien in your dream, this is usually an omen, a sign that there will be unexpected changes in your life. If you dream that you are the alien, this is symbolic that you will make some influential friends through an extracurricular activity.

Elves and fairies are frequently signs that your inner child is active, exploring and developing. They are usually harbingers of happiness and success.

When your subconscious delivers a dream with a fairy-tale subject or conclusion, it is probably encouraging you to do your utmost to ensure a positive outcome in your endeavors.

The image of a spiritual or religious figure in a dream might signify concern about your death or that of someone close to you. It might also signify your need to come to terms with sorrow (see also *Religion*, page 124).

A dream image of an angel suggests that your spiritual guide is attempting to communicate with you. Angel dreams are also considered very lucky—they can indicate that you will experience good fortune and protection from harm, especially if you are vigilant about listening to your higher self.

Dreaming of heaven or hell can indicate that you will experience substantial changes. Heaven is widely accepted as a dream symbol for justice, and also for long-term success. An image of hell often indicates that you have done something wrong for which you believe you deserve punishment, self-inflicted or otherwise. An image of flames being extinguished might express your belief that you don't deserve punishment. Dreaming of hell sometimes indicates that if you obtain some gain in life, you will do so at the expense of something you hold dear.

■ FOR **AMPUTATIONS**, SEE **ACCIDENTS**, PAGE 25.

■ FOR **ANGER**, SEE **ARGUMENTS**, PAGE 30.

ANIMALS

FOR **CATS**, SEE PAGE 41.
FOR **DEER**, SEE PAGE 52.
FOR **DOGS**, SEE PAGE 55.
FOR **REPTILES**, SEE PAGE 125.

When animals figure in dreams they are often symbols of "natural" feelings, which we may be trying to repress. Different species of animals are renowned for specific characteristics. The elephant, for example, is known to be methodical in character and have an impressive memory.

If you dream of an angry animal, it is likely that you are repressing your own anger. If you dream of a carefree animal, you might be suppressing a healthy yearning for more freedom and time to explore opportunities for personal growth. Nonaggressive animals in dreams generally signify your feelings of trust, contentment, and harmony. Playful animals typically signify feelings of joyful exuberance.

If you dream of an animal (usually a cat) sitting on top of or next to an object that is familiar to you, it is often the object, not the animal, to which you should pay attention. If you have seen the same animal in several dreams over months or perhaps years, it might be your animal totem or guide. If so, it might appear in your dreams to help you come to the correct conclusions or make the right decisions.

You might find that once you are aware of your animal totem, it will frequently manifest itself in your waking life in its physical form and in the form of other images you may happen upon, such as photographs or ornaments.

ELEPHANTS

These fascinating animals might frequent your dreams when you are concerned about remembering something important—during times of study, for example. Because they are large, slow-moving animals, elephants might also signify your concern about excess weight or a project that isn't moving as fast as you would like it to. However, the portly hippopotamus is a more common dream symbol for weight problems.

HORSES

The speed and grace of the galloping horse can indicate eagerness for change, and your anticipation of a new venture in life. Alternatively, it may be a sign that you are entering a very happy period in your life. A  white horse in a dream usually signifies fertility, prosperity, and success. This dream often appears during a woman's pregnancy, as she prepares for the birth.

LIONS

A dream of a powerful creature such as a lion or tiger generally signifies your inner strength, whether the animal in the dream is attacking or defending. Experiencing fear of these animals in a dream suggests that you fear what you see in yourself. A roaring lion indicates that you are taking a stand in life. A very still lion implies that you are prepared to respond to a new challenge.

MICE AND RATS

Dreaming of mice suggests that you are part of an efficient team or a close-knit family or group. It indicates that you are fitting into a group situation, be it family, work, or school. Rats suggest that you are feeling suspicious, or that you are an outsider, an observer rather than a participant. It is unusual to dream of rodents unless you are involved in certain matters, probably financial, in which you doubt the integrity of other parties.

MONKEYS

Monkey dreams typically reflect the mischievous, playful side of your nature.

RABBITS

A rabbit in a dream may herald the arrival of a new baby.

SHEEP

If you dream of sheep, you might be pleased by acceptance into a group or by the development of a new skill to a standard that equals that of people around you. The image of a shepherd traditionally relates to spiritual protection.

■ FOR **ANTIQUES**, SEE **FURNITURE,** PAGE 73.

ARGUMENTS

Dreaming that you are arguing is traditionally a good omen. However, if you see yourself losing control in an argument, your dream is telling you that you may be in danger of making a rash decision or being impulsive at the wrong time. Watch yourself over the next couple of days and count to ten before losing your temper.

Feeling angry in a dream concerning a particular person is a sign that you will reap some unexpected benefit from that person. If a person is angry at you for no reason, it is a warning of ill fortune. If you are angry because of an injustice, you will have good luck.

An argument with someone you do not know suggests that you will be lucky in a particular venture or project. Another possibility is that you are subconsciously attempting to convince yourself that you will not like someone who has just come into your life.

Interestingly, an accident that involves you dropping or breaking an object may be a sign that an argument is about to occur in your waking life, and that you will be the one to start it.

■ FOR **ARMCHAIR**, SEE **FURNITURE** ON PAGE 73.

DREAM TIP

Using dream-catchers to protect against nightmares

Many Native American tribes have used dream-catchers as a form of protection during sleep. Dream-catchers are usually a circle, made from rawhide or supple wood, and have woven "webs," like spiders' webs, on the inside. They are hung above the bed to filter out unnecessary dreams or nightmares, and to catch the dreams that we should remember. Dream-catchers are in plentiful supply at most new age stores—they are useful, beautiful, and well worth a try.

ARMOR

SEE ALSO **WAR**, PAGE 157.

Suits of armor are dream symbols that appear when you feel the need for greater protection, particularly if you are experiencing an emotional crisis. If you dream that you are wearing the armor yourself, you may need to check and recheck your financial circumstances and conserve your resources.

Dreaming that you are walking down a corridor decorated with suits of armor is believed to be a sign that you will soon receive awards and that your colleagues or peers will honor you or your work. Dreaming that you are in an armory, with men looking busy and purposeful and wearing suits of armor, is considered an omen of financial success.

ARMS AND AMMUNITION

Dreaming that you are going into battle or a meeting armed with ammunition indicates that you are preparing to come across obstacles in a particular project. When you are awake, see if you can identify what obstacles you may come across and whether or not you need to do more work to convince others about a particular part of the project or the project itself. Seeing yourself traveling while armed is thought to indicate that you will have to travel in the real world to achieve what you have set out to do.

DREAM TIP

What is sleep?

In sleep our conscious awareness becomes passive and our physical body slows down to rest, rejuvenate, and reenergize. It does this without the interference of the thinking, conscious mind. During sleep, the conscious mind allows the subconscious and higher conscious minds to take control. We will suffer from insomnia if we try to sleep while our conscious mind is still operating.

B

BAGS

Dreaming about a bag or suitcase is believed to have different meanings depending on what material the bag itself is made of. Also, look up any dream symbol for objects that the bag might contain, as they could be something that you will need or may represent an emotion, feeling or type of behavior you will need to constrain. The bag being full and heavy is believed to be a good omen for achieving what you desire—it indicates success.

If you dream of an empty paper bag, you may suffer from financial discomfort, but if the bag is made from cloth, you will find that your finances will take an upswing.

Naturally enough, bags and baggage are also indications that you are planning or will soon be taking an unexpected trip. Leather bags are an omen of a long, enjoyable holiday. If you dream that the bags are handled roughly, no matter what material they are made of, you will incur debts and will need to reconsider your finances.

BASEMENTS (INCLUDING CELLARS)

If you dream that you are in a dark basement, make sure in your waking world that you have enough information about a project you are planning to take on before you actually start it. You may have not been given all the facts you need.

Looking down into a basement in your dream indicates that you feel that there are things are going on around you that you don't understand, or that you are being excluded.

Similarly, dreaming of being in a dark cellar may indicate financial problems or that you fear that others will discover your secrets. However, if the cellar is well stocked, your business will expand and your projects will succeed.

BELLS

Dreaming that you are hearing bells may indicate that you will soon be receiving unfavorable news. Hearing church bells ringing is believed to be a sign that your enemies may be plotting against you. Bells are dream symbols of warning, letting you know that a disturbance or disruption may become a problem for you or your work.

BETRAYALS

Feeling distressed, upset, lonely, or betrayed in a dream signifies that you are lacking self-confidence at the moment. A feeling of exposure often indicates hurt feelings that you haven't revealed to those who distressed you.

DREAM FACT

How your subconscious mind works

The subconscious mind has several roles. First, it is the storehouse for memories, emotions, habits, and behavioral patterns. It is the repository for your past experiences, beliefs, values, and identity, and creates reactions based on this stored information. It is highly adaptive and "runs" your life as best it can with the choices it has available.

Second, it is responsible for the running of your physical body, with all its complex systems and chemical processes. Luckily, the subconscious mind can handle and process innumerable items of information simultaneously without becoming weighed down. It only stores, sorts, and filters data.

Third, the subconscious mind helps mediate between the conscious and the higher conscious minds. One of its main functions is to communicate directly with the higher conscious mind. The subconscious mind receives information from the higher consciousness as intuition, and then passes it to the conscious mind.

BIRDS

SEE ALSO **FLYING**, PAGE 72.

Flying represents freedom. So when you dream of flying birds or animals, including humans, you may have broken free of restriction, self-imposed or otherwise. You are now free to explore, to move in any direction you choose. Such dreams are common when you are formulating new ideas or investigating your own possibilities and potential.

Birds have always been powerfully spiritual symbols. If they feature in your dreams, it may indicate a need to reflect on the direction you are currently taking in your life. Some birds embody a particular widely acknowledged meaning: the owl represents wisdom, the eagle represents silent strength and clear sight, and the crow represents sense of direction (nomadic tribes often followed the path of the crow when looking for food, water, or wintering grounds).

Images of birds might also be prophetic. They can indicate that something very powerful is coming into your life or that issues that currently concern you are about to be resolved.

Dream images of birds might also convey a warning to the dreamer. A dream of an owl flying across your path, for example, means you should slow down and be more cautious, as there could be something dangerous ahead.

A dream of a bird with eggs signifies wealth and gain. A dream of a nest without eggs indicates a fear of loss—the loss of a relationship or the loss of your sense of self. Cackling chickens or quacking ducks often represent unwelcome information, repetition, or extreme frustration at not being able to make yourself heard among others. It is traditionally believed that if a woman dreams of a bird with beautifully colored plumage, she will, in the real world, attract a handsome, wealthy husband!

BIRTHS

A dream of birth, the coming into being of any life form, frequently indicates your emerging awareness and understanding of yourself and others, your self-acceptance, the beginning of something new in your life, or the development of an idea.

To dream of the birth of a child, even if it is a traumatic experience, might represent the nurturing of growth within yourself, and being in control of your own vulnerability and strength. A birth might also indicate that major, positive changes are imminent for you or someone close to you.

People preparing to wed often dream of a birth—it is a symbol of a new beginning and an indication of their excitement and acceptance of the changes marriage will bring to their lives. Dreaming that you are assisting in a birth is believed to mean that you are about to experience great joy and happiness in you own life.

Dreaming of a miscarriage or an abortion suggests either a subconscious purging of some deep emotion, a seriously mistaken view, or absolute denial of a person or a matter of great significance to you.

BLOOD

Blood featured in a dream could be a warning that you are doing too much; you may be exhausting yourself and you may not be able to focus on any one thing properly. Traditionally, blood in dreams is believed to be an omen of disappointment. This disappointment may be caused by not taking care of yourself or your project so that you miss the details that would have ensured success.

Bleeding from a wound or the appearance of blood on your clothes may indicate a number of misfortunes, such as an estrangement from your best friend, the failure of a love affair, or a person blocking your advancement at work.

BODIES

Your body stores your feelings. If you are stressed, your stress may manifest in physical aches and pains, or the body may become the main feature of a dream. It might be that in your wakened state you are discounting the importance of your emotions. To protect you from this error of judgment, your subconscious might use images of the body to reflect your emotional state. For example, if your body feels heavy in a dream, you might be feeling overburdened in some or all parts of your life.

Experiencing your body shape in a dream as quite different from its actual shape can be interpreted in many ways. A woman whose breasts seem larger in her dream than in reality might be experiencing a desire to breast-feed or feeling a physical tenderness toward others. A man whose genitals seem smaller in his dreams than in reality might be feeling vulnerable.

Seeing your body as a body of the opposite gender might mean that you are tuning in to that side of your nature in your quest for emotional balance. A strong, dominant male might be reminded of the gentle side of his nature in a dream where his body becomes female. A soft, gentle woman might see herself as a man in a dream to remind her of her strength.

The various parts of the body have their own significance, as do injuries to these areas (see *Accidents*, page 25). For example, a female figure with a very rounded belly in a dream is typically a sign of

prosperity or financial gain. Images of strange markings on the stomach might relate to your attempts to release anger or frustration and may indicate that your emotions are temporarily overwhelming you.

BOOKS

Books often appear in dreams when you are learning and developing, or when you feel there are issues that you want to understand or should become familiar with. Different types of books have traditionally been associated with particular meanings. For example, reading a textbook is believed to presage worldly wealth, whereas reading a novel is an omen that you will lose a friend.

Dreaming of writing books is thought to be an indication that you will engage in a venture that will waste your time and money. However, the act of writing or images of words generally reflects a desire to understand and to be clearly understood. An image of ornate or archaic lettering often indicates the reactivation of your creativity, your sense of beauty, or your appreciation of nature—perhaps one or all of these once flowed through your life but has been suppressed. It might be a sign to free your mind from the daily grind.

Curiously, dreaming of bookcases full of books is traditionally considered a sign of a lack of care in your real world. However, an almost empty bookcase is an omen of good fortune.

DREAM FACT

One of the first dream psychologists:
Sigmund Freud (1856–1939)

In his work *The Interpretation of Dreams* (1899), the Austrian psychoanalyst Sigmund Freud said: "I shall bring forward proof that there is a psychological technique which makes it possible to interpret dreams." Freud felt that all dreams were driven by our sexual libido. He believed that dreams are "the royal road to the unconscious," coded messages that come from the subconscious to advise of repressed desires and instincts. His hypothesis about dreams was associated with illness rather than wellness, but he paved the way for us to search our dreams for information about ourselves.

BRAINS

Dreaming of an exposed brain might represent deep thought, confusion, or uncertainty, or it may represent finally understanding an issue or completing a task.

■ FOR **BRIDE, BRIDEGROOM,** AND **BRIDESMAID,** SEE **MARRIAGES,** PAGE 102, AND **WEDDINGS,** PAGE 159.

BRIDGES

A bridge is a common symbol of transition or growth. If you find you are on one side of a bridge, you might be preparing yourself for changes that you feel uncertain about. If you are in the middle of the bridge, you are probably growing as a person and about to enter a new period in your life. If you have reached the far side of a bridge, you might have conquered a fear or resolved an issue that you had reservations about.

Take note of how long you take crossing the bridge. You will be fortunate if you do not take too long to cross the bridge: this indicates that you will—or are just about to—resolve an emotional problem that has been worrying you. Also, observe whether or not the bridge is being repaired; if it is, it may indicate that your plans for change are not in good condition and need more attention.

■ FOR **BURGLARIES,** SEE **CRIMES,** PAGE 48.

BURIALS

Seeing yourself buried is often a sign that you are feeling the pressure of some situation in your life. You may be feeling overwhelmed by concerns such as finances and workload pressures. When you wake up, perhaps you should work on rearranging your schedule to give yourself more breathing space.

Such a dream could also indicate that you are grappling with whether or not to join a venture that could be slightly shady or unethical. Your dream is warning you that you may pay dearly for going ahead with the venture—mud sticks!

If you dream of a hole in the ground, such as an empty burial plot, you might be entering a situation in your waking life that you expect to lose control of.

Oddly enough, dreaming of a burial is traditionally believed to be an omen that you will soon be attending a wedding, or that you will receive some other joyful news, such as the birth of a child or the graduation of a teenager.

■ FOR **BUTTERFLIES**, SEE **INSECTS**, PAGE 87.

DREAM TIP

The brain in action

The electrical and chemical activity of the brain during sleep can be viewed using an electroencephalograph (EEG), a machine which records brain waves and shows areas of brain activity. The brain appears to create dreams through random electrical activity. The brain stem sends out electrical impulses approximately every 90 minutes. As the left brain—the brain's analytical part—tries to make sense of these signals, it forms a dream. The way to understand the dream best is to see it symbolically. A literal or realistic message does not usually exist.

CAMERAS

Being photographed in a dream often indicates a feeling that you are on display. Photographing others usually reflects your conscious

efforts to remember information, and may indicate that you are having difficulties absorbing information. Dreaming of a camera may also be a sign that, emotionally, you are hanging on to the present and not going forward into the future.

CARS

Being in a car with others suggests that you are developing friendships and alliances and a broader understanding of life in the process. However, if the car trip is frustrating, it may be that you are feeling that you are out of control in your waking life. If the car is like a sport vehicle that is navigating bumpy roads, it may be that you are surmounting obstacles in your waking life. Being either the driver or passenger in a car going to a meeting with others suggests that you might be about to make new friends.

Dreaming of a car crash usually represents a conflict or argument with a friend or friends. Dreams of accidents between people and moving vehicles generally reflect fears that a present involvement, perhaps a personal relationship, will entail damaging conflict or will not meet your expectations. It might also indicate feelings that others are enjoying life in ways that are closed to you.

CATS

SEE ALSO **ANIMALS**, PAGES 28-29.

Domestic cats in a dream are generally warnings to put aside self-pity and counter adversity in your life. Cats moving around you might indicate an awakening of your spiritual growth and sensitivity; a fighting cat suggests that the dreamer is experiencing internal conflict. Black cats generally signify superstition and uncertainty, and often appear when you are having difficulty determining the difference between fantasy and reality.

CELEBRATIONS

Parties and celebrations in dreams reflect the joy of success and relaxation. You might be feeling relief that a time or event that you were unsure of or feared has passed. Feeling virtuous or happy in a dream can be a sign that you have lived up to your own expectations or standards in your waking life.

- FOR **CELLARS**, SEE **BASEMENTS**, PAGE 32.
- FOR **CHAIRS**, SEE **FURNITURE**, PAGE 73.
- FOR **CHAKRAS**, SEE **COLORS**, PAGES 44-47.

CHASING (INCLUDING RUNNING)

Dreams of chasing usually mean you are avoiding something. A dream of someone chasing you might reflect the fear that a lie you have told is catching up with you. Dreams of running imply avoidance, confusion, and an inability to deal with the situation. Dreaming of running while you are not touching the ground suggests that you are stuck in a situation and are feeling helpless, or perhaps you need to take life at a slower pace but are finding it difficult to do so. It might also mean that you are finding it difficult to learn patience.

CHILDREN

To a female, a dream of small and well-behaved children might signify her knowledge of solutions to her current problems. To a male, such a dream usually signifies matters of responsibility or issues involving actual children. Difficulties with children in a

dream may represent your difficulties with either the children in your life or your own inner child. Children running away from you might reflect your feelings of inadequacy or uncertainty in some situations. A dream of children running toward you often indicates that you feel accepted for yourself, or that you could be successful in resolving a disagreement between others.

CHOCOLATES, CANDY, AND ICE CREAM

Dreaming that you are eating candy commonly represents a self-reward or a treat. However, striped candy might indicate some physical disorder. For a woman, this may be hormonal; for a man, it may mean a problem with the immune system. Dreaming that you are eating ice cream usually signifies success and an acknowledgment that you have done well. Eating chocolate might indicate a better than expected resolution to a worrisome situation.

CIGARETTES

Smoking a cigarette in a dream is usually connected to anxiety, but it may reflect the fact that you have decided to give up smoking (or another damaging habit) but are having problems with it.

CLOCKS

Dream clocks usually reflect your fears about time, such as the worry that you might be unpunctual or that there are not enough hours in the day. You may be experiencing a feeling that you are always rushing.

CLOTHING

SEE ALSO **NAKEDNESS**, PAGE 112.
FOR **ZIPPERS**, SEE PAGE 163.

When you see yourself without clothes in a dream, your subconscious is probably reflecting your fear of being vulnerable.

When you see yourself wearing lots of warm clothing, it might be that you are ill, or would like some time on your own. Brightly colored or patterned clothes in a dream suggest that you want to be noticed or heeded by others. If you are dressed in colorful pajamas, you are probably in a state of inner peace and harmony.

Wearing dark or reflective clothing in a dream suggests that in your waking state you attempt to conceal your true self from others.

Stained clothes in a dream usually represent something you can't eliminate from your life. Stockings with runs or socks with holes often herald an invasion of your personal space. A dream where you are worried about odd socks might be a reminder that you can't please everyone at once.

An adult man wearing short pants in a dream often indicates feelings of vulnerability or fear of exposure.

A dream in which you are wearing clothes that are too small for you indicates the presence in your life of an attitude, object, or structure that you feel you have outgrown. A dream in which you wear clothes that are too large for you might mean you are struggling with a new idea, with promotion or study, or with growing into a new space.

The image of a hat in a dream might occur just before you ask for a salary increase or just after you get a promotion or new job. If the hat is bright or large, it usually reflects your desire to attract, show off, or be seen. If it is small or demure, it indicates that you want to blend in with other people. Wearing gloves in a dream suggests that you feel vulnerable and are attempting to protect yourself.

COINS

Losing a copper coin in a dream usually indicates lack of confidence; finding one represents an increased level of self-esteem. If you find a small silver coin in a dream, you might be about to receive money through a stroke of unexpected good luck. A large silver coin is often a symbol for inspiration or of the need to make changes in your life.

COLORS (INCLUDING THE CHAKRAS)

When your subconscious brings color to your dreams, it usually wants your conscious mind to focus clearly on the dream—to remember it all, not just parts of it. When you dream in color, you are often opening up to your total being. You might be starting to know and understand who you are, how you affect other people, what is necessary in your life, what gives you great joy and happiness, and what creates harmony in your life. Dreaming in color does not mean that everything is the one color. If your dream is dominated by one color, there may be a significant correlation to the chakra with which that color is associated.

The major element of the life force within the human body is the electromagnetic energy field, which permeates the body. The body has hundreds of energy centers that service the various muscles and organs. These are the focal points of acupuncture. However, there are seven major chakra centers or energy centers. The chart opposite shows you their location, color, and function.

If, for example, you dream of a forest of trees with blue flowers among them, you would find, by considering the chakras associated with green and blue, that issues of the heart, unconditional love and communication are currently at the forefront of your subconscious.

RED

Red can represent a deep emotion or a blocked problem. It might mean that the body is undergoing healing, or that the dreamer is physically very active and energetic. It can relate to sensual experience, sexual fantasies, and personal attraction.

Dreaming in red is also a way of releasing feelings in a dream state that you are having difficulty dealing with in your waking state. Red can be expansive, indicating hope and potential success. The lighter or brighter the red, the more balanced you feel about a situation in your life. If a soft, gentle pink features in a dream, you may be getting excited about something, perhaps an upcoming promotion or success in your career or a relationship.

The deeper and more prevalent the red in any dream, the stronger the emotion and the more likely it is to be a warning, or to represent concerns or uncertainties about the subject of the dream. In a dream about employment, for example, dark shades of red usually mean that you are striving for success but, perhaps, your confidence base is not secure—you may be concerned with external influences or other people's opinions of you. You will find that the deeper the color, the more ingrained are those concerns.

If the red-tinged dream is very abstract or somewhat frightening, your subconscious is trying to make you stop ignoring the problem.

ORANGE

This color represents the level where you store your emotions, so orange in your dreams represents stored nervous energy or anxieties. It suggests that traumatic events have affected you. A dream featuring orange could be a signal that these stored feelings

CHAKRA	LOCATION	COLOR	FUNCTION
Base	Base of spine	Red	Expectations, physical energy, physical restrictions
Spleen	Just below the navel	Orange	Trauma, shock, recall
Solar plexus	Just above the navel	Yellow	Subconscious thoughts
Heart	Center of chest	Green	Empathy, emotion, unconditional love
Throat	Throat	Blue	Communication
Brow or Third Eye	Center of forehead	Indigo	Higher consciousness, intuition, awareness
Crown	Top and center of head	Violet	Spirituality

will have an effect on your health by creating an imbalance in your system. Such a dream could signify the onset of a virus, or mean that you are exhausted and in need of some form of rest, meditation, or exercise to expel nervous energy. Dreaming in shades of orange may also indicate that, at this point, real understanding about what you are feeling is out of your reach.

Orange in a dream could also be a warning that an upcoming situation or event may not be as successful for you as you would like it to be, possibly because your anxieties interfere with your actions. Such a dream gives you the chance to reevaluate matters and your approach to them.

Whether the color orange means clarity, physical health, or success depends on the context of your dream.

YELLOW

A golden-yellow dream usually signifies great opportunity and achievement. If your dream focuses on your career, golden yellow often represents expansion. It might indicate that you possess great confidence, are making the right choice for yourself at this time, and will probably be very successful.

Bright yellow dreams could relate to the mental activity that governs your life. This color indicates that you are making progress in either your conscious or subconscious life, and that you are approaching life with the correct emphasis. Like the sun, shining yellow is a sign that you are in harmony with yourself and your life.

GREEN

Whatever the shade, green is an emotional color. A vibrant, lush green in a dream can reinforce that you are in love with life and your place in it, and in emotional balance with other people. It may also bode well for your good health and physical vitality. In deeper tones, green can signify jealousy or uncertainty concerning others. It is a confronting color that seeks to enhance your ability to understand both your own and others' perspectives and to make balanced decisions.

BLUE

This is the color of communication, representing clarity and the ability to express yourself well in any situation. In a dream, it suggests that you are either about to or should express your emotions. This is an excellent color to see in a dream, because it indicates that you are in a position that necessitates a great deal of communication. Blue also signifies alignment with your inner self and a restoration of focus.

INDIGO

Indigo is the color of thought and reflection. An indigo dream indicates that you are or should be practicing self-analysis. This is a color that might also indicate restlessness with your current life. It could represent a spiritual quest, a search for more challenges or new directions, or a need to reevaluate your goals.

VIOLET

Having passed through the stages of reflection marked by indigo, violet brings you into a state of advanced awareness. Dreams in this color may reflect your understanding of what changes you need to incorporate into your life and how to make them happen. Violet and lavender both indicate great clarity in all issues of life, and are very spiritual colors; dreams in which these colors dominate should encourage you to look at the spiritual aspects of your life.

DREAM TIP

Noise from the outside

Noises from outside will readily be incorporated into the dream state. Here is a pertinent dream report: "I was asleep, and dreaming about flying over the ocean. It was very dark, and silent, and I was afraid. Then suddenly I was listening to a song, one I'd heard before but couldn't quite place, and I relaxed. As I relaxed I began to fall, and a moment later I woke up out of my dream. I realized I had been dreaming, and that the song playing on the clock radio beside my bed had become part of my dream."

CRIMES

A dream in which you are being murdered suggests that someone is suffocating your ideas and you feel unable to express yourself properly. There may also be some kind of threat arising in your life, or you may feel an intangible fear developing. Witnessing a murder in a dream is an indication that you may see changes in your environment that you will not be particularly keen about. If you dream that you are killing someone, you are probably experiencing severe emotional stress—you will need to take time to relax. It is important to keep control of your temper in the next couple of days.

Being stabbed in a dream indicates that you are upset and uncertain; being shot suggests that your feelings have been hurt—you may have taken something someone has said or done a little too much to heart. Being deliberately run over may indicate that other people are getting involved in activities in which you feel unable to participate.

A dream featuring a policeman or policewoman, however, might relate to money, inheritance, or legal matters, or signify a fear of the consequences of your actions. A police officer in your dream can also indicate that you will receive some help from an authority figure for a problem you are experiencing.

A dream about a robbery might represent your fear that something you value may be taken away. Traditionally, dreaming about a robbery or a burglary is believed to have two contrary meanings: (1) that if you lose something of importance in your dream, you will receive something in the real world that you want, and (2) that dreams of losing money during a robbery or burglary are a warning that you need to take more care with your finances.

DREAM TIP

Totem animals

Many people turn to totem animals when they need guidance or help in the area of the animal's special abilities. For instance, before going to sleep you might request the assistance of a deer totem if you feel you urgently need to find safety and security.

■ FOR **CROWS**, SEE **BIRDS**, PAGE 34.

CURSES

Dreaming about curses is an indication that you feel that you will lose the respect of your peers or family. Traditionally, if you are the one doing the cursing, you will suffer humiliation and misfortune. However, if you are the one being cursed, you will instead gain in social stature and may even acquire authoritative new friends.

CURTAINS

Curtains blowing in the wind are frequently symbols of inner harmony and higher spiritual learning. If you dream that you are putting up curtains or selecting some new curtains, this is an indication that you may have an increase in the number of friends and family that visit your house.

CUSHIONS

Dreaming of a large number of cushions surrounding you may indicate that you are feeling stifled and have abandoned a path that may be difficult, though very rewarding. If the cushions in your dream are looking torn and shabby, it means that you may find that a small investment brings you modest returns.

■ FOR **CUTTING**, SEE **KNIVES**, PAGE 95.
■ FOR **CYCLONES**, SEE **WEATHER**, PAGE 159.

D

■ FOR **DAGGERS**, SEE **KNIVES**, PAGE 95.

DANCING

Dancing in a dream suggests happiness, excitement and enthusiasm, stability, and an internal balance. If it is ballet, it is likely that you are entering a period of self-approval and a flourishing of the creative side of your personality or that of someone close to you. It also can signify that you will have the confidence to enter into social circles that previously seemed closed to you because you were shy or had a misplaced sense of humility.

Dreams where you are watching someone dance are also fortuitous. For example, if you see children dancing, this is often an indication that you will receive unexpected news that will bring you joy. Watching people dancing in a ballroom signifies that you are increasingly enjoying a sense of freedom, harmony, and balance with your friends, family, and/or colleagues. Watching people dancing in a disco or nightclub signifies that a relationship that seemed to be flagging will be revitalized.

DARNING

SEE ALSO **CLOTHING**, PAGE 43.

Dreaming that you are darning a piece of clothing suggests that you will be successful in tackling the issues that have made you reject a friendship or that have caused a rift in your family. Traditionally, a dream about darning signifies that you will be introduced to a new person who will become your friend. If in your dream you are watching someone else darning, though, the traditional meaning is that you may become the subject of gossip. Further information may be given to you if you notice what type of garment you are darning.

DEATHS

Like the Death Card in a Tarot deck, death in a dream does not represent the actual death of a person. Instead, it represents the ending of the old and the beginning of the new. It can be a sign of release, and of the acceptance of change in oneself or another.

A dream about death could suggest the elimination of fears and phobias, or it could herald a new ability to take the initiative, perhaps in the form of an overdue confrontation with someone. Such a dream might also mean that you are coming to terms with childhood experiences or that you are outgrowing childish or unrealistic attitudes.

It is quite common for parents of growing children to dream of their children's deaths. Such dreams usually occur when the parent has reservations about the change in the relationship with their children as they emerge from childhood to adulthood.

DREAM REPORT

A death dream

When my brother was in his early thirties, he was dying. While he was going through the torment of his illness, I dreamed that I could see my brother in an above-ground swimming pool. He was in it up to his chest and trying to get out. There didn't appear to be any water in the pool, and he was leaning on the side holding out his hands. My mother was crying and trying to lift him over the side, and they were both exhausted.

The family was all gathered around, just watching and crying. When both he and my mother decided to rest, and it seemed he had no bodily strength left, he simply put his hands together and lifted himself straight up. He looked serene and peaceful. I awoke crying. The next day I was told he had passed on.

This dream was a metaphor for how he had struggled against death. Once my brother was released, his letting go was peaceful and beautiful.

DEBTS

Dreaming that you are in debt is an indication that you are concerned about your business finances and need to take stock of your money. Spend some time coming to terms with your monetary situation. Do not try to ignore any problems—they will not go away.

A dream that you have repaid your debts traditionally means that you will enjoy a fruitful time in the immediate future. If you dream that someone has repaid his or her debt to you, you may need to watch out for losses to your own finances.

DECEPTIONS

Dreaming that someone is deceiving you and that you find them out is a very fortunate dream, indicating that you are able to assess your situation accurately, particularly with regard to your financial matters. If in your dream you are the person doing the deceiving, when you wake up, reconsider any business actions you may be planning that involve cutting corners. Your dream may be a warning that you will be found out and that you will suffer the consequences of your actions.

DEER

Traditional dream interpretations have linked the symbol of a deer with loss of friendships, business partnerships, engagements, and marriages, as well as with legal troubles that might land you in court. If you dream of a deer in its natural habitat, you may find that you will get an opportunity to become friends with a quick-witted individual or bring that aspect out in yourself. It is considered a bad omen to see a caged or dead deer—this indicates disappointment or strong unhappiness.

DISAPPEARANCES

When a person or object seems to vanish in your dreams, this is an indication that you will most probably be given a lot of information or conflicting advice in the near future about a particular project or person. However, your dream shows you that you already have the ability to clear the issue from view and not be overcome by it.

DISASTERS

No matter whether you are in the middle of it or are merely a witness, dreams of major disasters—either in your life or as a major event affecting your neighborhood, country, or the world—often in fact presage a period of improvement, even prosperity. Disaster dreams are traditionally thought to be contrary dreams—their meaning is the opposite of what they are about. They can also indicate sudden and out-of-control upheavals in your life: turning points and opportunities in new directions.

DISCUSSIONS

Endless discussions in a dream signify that there are a lot of issues or various people's agendas clouding the particular topic that the discussions seem to be about. Take this as an indication that there is unnecessary delay being generated concerning a project or relationship in your real life and that you must not be influenced by any of these discussions—they are irrelevant to the issue. This is a good opportunity to listen to your own intuition when making a decision—you can rely on your own ability to judge the situation correctly.

DISEASES

SEE ALSO **MEDICAL MATTERS**, PAGE 103.

A dream image of your body enduring fever or other symptoms of disease usually relates to self-punishment. Perhaps you know something about yourself that distresses you or you have been offended by someone else. Such a dream might also be warning you to pay more attention to your health. A dream of a heart attack might be a subconscious warning that you should take better care of your body because it is being adversely affected by stress. To dream about a doctor or a healer might reflect a desire to be looked after or healed in some way. It may be a message that you or someone you know needs to consult a physician.

Anyone who is extremely ill should pay particular attention to recurring and vivid dreams. Sometimes there will also be a series of dreams that progress in some kind of sequence. Also note that:

- a dream that is puzzling often indicates a need for more information;
- a dream that is frightening may relate to fears about the illness or about dying;
- a dream full of frustration and anxiety may mean that the ailing person is worried about family, arrangements, and the expense of the illness.

DREAM FACT

Sharing dreams can help the dying

Dreams can have a particularly powerful meaning for the dying. People who are near death often have profound dreams containing vital information that can allow them to complete the process of dying. Being able to talk about dreams or visions is therapeutic for people who are dying—it helps them understand their own concerns. Encourage people in this situation to tell you the details, and help them interpret their dreams. Sometimes a death dream may come to someone other than the dying person, perhaps a close friend. Understanding this dream may allow them to give understanding and assistance to the dying person.

DIVORCES

A dream about an ex-partner might indicate that there are still unresolved issues between you or that you feel there is something you haven't discussed. Alternatively, the dream might be a final farewell in which you are acknowledging the end of the relationship. If you are still married, this is traditionally regarded as a contrary dream: it signals that your marriage is strong and impervious to outside threats.

DOGS

SEE ALSO **ANIMALS**, PAGES 28-29.

Dogs usually signify loyalty, protection and unconditional love. Traditionally, dogs in dreams indicate good luck in your choice of friends. However, in some dreams they can indicate that the dreamer is feeling lonely, unloved, and not accepted for themselves. Sometimes dogs appear in your dreams when you have argued with a loved one or have had little contact with them recently.

If you dream of a dog in difficulty, it means your own comfort level is under threat from the people or events in your life. Barking, playful dogs indicate that your own mood is fun seeking and companionable, or that you will soon enjoy an exciting event or special occasion in which you are the focus of attention. A dog barking in a harsh way indicates the possibility of legal issues becoming a threat to you.

If the dog is snarling and is acting in a threatening manner, this is a warning that you may experience deceit from a friend. However, if a very large and powerful dog looms over you and you do not feel threatened by it, you will have the help of a powerful friend in your endeavors.

■ FOR **DOLPHINS**, SEE **FISH AND OTHER SEA CREATURES**, PAGES 68-69.

DOORS

Open doorways typically invite the conscious mind to explore opportunities being offered in life. Passing through a doorway in a dream represents embarking upon a new and exciting period in your life, a period that might herald new developments in your career, relationships, or home.

Running through a doorway and banging a door behind you might be a sign that you are weighing your positive attitude against your uncertainties to determine what the outcome of a situation may be. Being chased through doors might indicate that you need to escape from someone in your waking life. Locking a door behind you suggests that this situation is overwhelming, and that you are unable to deal with it at the moment.

Dreaming of a closed door is often an expression of indecision or despair; it may also indicate that you are concerned about whether or not opportunities will present themselves. If a closed door is bolted, you might be feeling locked in to the life you have created and unable to change it.

A door lock that has no key suggests either that you find it difficult to express emotions or that you desire privacy. Ringing a doorbell indicates that you will soon have the opportunity to make friends with an exciting new person. If you hear a doorbell ringing and respond by opening the door, you are ready to engage in new opportunities.

DRINKS

Dreams where you are drinking a particular substance usually concern your emotional life. Cow's milk traditionally signifies motherhood and the abundance of life. Milk in a jug often represents self-made wealth and success, self-sufficiency, and satisfaction. A dream about drinking milk is symbolic of gaining happiness and success. Dreaming of drinking sweet drinks is believed to presage an exciting new love affair. Drinking water is believed to be a good omen for students, indicating that they will achieve their goals through the acquisition of knowledge.

DROWNING

SEE ALSO **UNDERWATER**, PAGE 150.

Drowning is traditionally symbolic of the loss of money. If you own a business, dreaming that you or a business partner is drowning can indicate that you fear you are close to bankruptcy.

A dream about drowning can also mean you feel that you are being swamped by emotional problems you can't handle, or that you are dealing with a long-term sorrow. If you are rescued in your dream, you will not suffer financial loss—a friend may intervene in real life and help you avoid the loss. If you dream that you are rescuing a drowning friend, your friend may well get a promotion at work.

DREAM FACT

One of the first dream psychologists:
Carl Gustav Jung (1875–1961)

A world-renowned psychologist and one-time protégé of Sigmund Freud, Carl Jung went beyond Freud in recognizing a sublevel of the subconscious mind. He postulated that the human psyche has an impersonal level as well as the personal one. The impersonal level, which he called the "collective unconscious," contains archetypes—remnants from the evolution of the human psyche. Jung believed that we draw on archetypes in our dreams and that our subconscious mind then individualizes them to match our specific natures. Jung believed that focusing when we are awake on the symbols in a dream would reveal the dream and its conflicts to the conscious mind. He also emphasized the importance of a person's present experiences to the dream. Jung was perhaps the first to have a theory that we are dreaming all the time, and that only the distraction of our waking life leaves us unaware of the fact. He also believed that the human psyche is constantly progressing toward its goal of wholeness and maturity. Understanding and controlling our dreams enable us to move us closer to that goal.

E

■ FOR **EAGLES**, SEE **BIRDS**, PAGE 34.

■ FOR **EARRINGS**, SEE **JEWELRY**, PAGES 90–91,
AND **RINGS**, PAGE 125.

EARS

Dreaming of ears is usually symbolic of not hearing, listening, or understanding. A dream in which you are aware of other people's ears is thought to be an omen that you will soon hear some extraordinary news.

Ears also can be an indication that your friends may not be listening to you, or that you have some friends who are not as trustworthy as you had first thought. When you dream of ears, take some time to see if you feel confident that your friends are listening to you and that you are listening to them. If you act to remedy any lack of attention that you have been exhibiting toward a particular friend, you may prevent the friendship from souring.

EARTHQUAKES

SEE ALSO **DISASTERS**, PAGE 53.

Dreaming of an earthquake might mean that your sleep is being disturbed by outside noises. Dream images of your whole environment shaking under your feet may also indicate that you feel your whole world is changing in a radical way, making it difficult for you to keep your footing and feel settled. The dream suggests that in order to overcome the challenges in your life you may first need to work toward feeling fully grounded and stable. Traditionally, earthquake dreams are contrary dreams—they are thought to be a sign that you will overcome your problems.

EATING AND PREPARING FOOD

SEE ALSO **CHOCOLATES, CANDY, AND ICE CREAM**, PAGE 42.

Preparing food is a common dream symbol of creativity and purpose in life. Seeing yourself at a dinner party might reflect a need to be more sociable in your waking life. A dream where you are eating with a group of your friends is traditionally seen as an omen of good fortune, while eating by yourself can be an indication that you are feeling lonely and need to reconnect with your friends.

Eating with pleasure might mean acceptance of your physical appearance. To dream of huge quantities of food or that your appetite is insatiable suggests that you worry about your weight and about possible weight gain.

If you dream of delicious food, you may be anticipating a pleasant event. If you are eating a decadent dessert in your dream, you might be feeling the need to act spontaneously and to enjoy something out of the ordinary.

Dreaming of unfamiliar food suggests that you feel uncomfortable with your colleagues and acquaintances.

Eggs usually represent new people coming into your life. Fried eggs might represent fitting into a situation or understanding a situation for what it really is. Broken eggs usually represent vulnerability and uncertainty in personal relationships.

Green fruit in a dream usually signifies that you know the outcome of a situation and are preparing for the final stages. Unusual fruit generally represents doubt, confusion, or a feeling that something is not quite right in your life.

Nuts tend to feature in the dreams of people who are accumulating money to finance a particular goal. Such dream images might also be a message from your subconscious that you are successfully identifying all your priorities.

ELECTRICITY

A dream about electricity is connected with the flow of positive energy in your life. Dreaming that the electricity cuts out and you are plunged into darkness indicates that you may be feeling that you are wasting your energy and time on a project—perhaps

it will not give you an advantage commensurate with the effort you have put into it.

Take particular note in your dream of what you were doing immediately before the power failure—this may give you an indication of what particular project or relationship your dream is telling you is a waste of time.

If you are the one who switches off the electricity, it may be because you feel run-down and need to conserve your energy. When you wake up, consider having a general checkup with your doctor and taking a bit more of a break than you have been allowing yourself lately.

Dreaming of unprotected electricity is traditionally considered a warning. If you are shocked by a live wire in a dream, you will soon be confronted by some startling news in real life. If you dream that wires are crossed, you may have been careless in business and could soon be facing some loss.

ELEVATORS AND ESCALATORS

Dreaming that you are traveling up an elevator or an escalator is believed to be an indication that you are going "up" in life. However, dreaming that you are traveling downward may indicate that there are some reversals and obstacles in your life.

Take note of what you are wearing or carrying and whether or not you are with someone while you are in the elevator—this may help you decide whether your dream symbol is connected to a particular project or relationship.

EMBROIDERY

Dreaming that you are doing embroidery is considered a sign of good fortune; it suggests that your life is becoming settled and relaxed. You now have the time to beautify your environment and the energy to be creative.

ENGAGEMENTS

SEE ALSO **MARRIAGES**, PAGE 102, AND **WEDDINGS**, PAGE 160.

Traditionally, dreaming of getting engaged or having your engagement broken is an omen of family or relationship troubles ahead. Focus first on the person you are engaged to in the dream— if that person is known to you in the real world, take particular care to avoid controversial issues with them for a time.

ENTRAPMENT

SEE ALSO **SCREAMING**, PAGE 130.

Symbols of entrapment and imprisonment often appear in your dreams when you feel constrained by necessities in your life, such as keeping a job just to pay the bills. Dreams about various forms of entrapment are common to new parents, who have growing family responsibilities and are uncertain about the limitations this will place on them.

Children resisting behavioral boundaries set by their parents might have dreams of entrapment. Screaming in such a dream is often an indication that you are unable to release frustration.

EYES

A dream of eyes that are bright, alert or otherwise attractive usually means that you are communicating well with others. Seeing glazed eyes might be a sign that someone doesn't understand what you are trying to convey.

F

FACES

The image of a face in a dream generally represents an expectation and your uncertainty about it. Traditionally, dreaming of a pleasant-faced person is considered a good omen, but if the face of the person is grotesque and disturbing, you may be facing some obstacles and losses. A dirty face usually signifies a situation not working out as well as you anticipated. Curiously, chocolate on the face might indicate a better than expected resolution to a worrying situation. A smiling face indicates the dawn of understanding and harmony.

FALLING

Experiencing falling in a dream suggests that you do not feel in control or that you need to extract yourself from some situation. Such dreams often occur when you are unable to determine the cause of your uncertainty or are postponing choices or decisions. Falling may also indicate that you are afraid of losing your position in life.

If you dream that you fall but are able to get up, you will be able to overcome your fears or obstacles.

You may also have falling dreams when you go to sleep worrying that you won't wake when you should, or you feel anxious about being late. It is common to dream of falling when you need to wake up and go to the bathroom.

For a child, dreaming of falling may represent fear that they will lose the love of a parent, particularly if the child has gone to sleep after being in trouble with a parent.

FAME

SEE ALSO **FACES**, PAGE 62.

If you dream you are a famous person, you might be imposing limitations on yourself in your waking life that are preventing you from fulfilling your potential—you should trust in your abilities. Another interpretation is that you are trying to reach for something that is beyond your grasp; it may be that you are seeking results or goals too quickly and that you need to move more slowly toward your ultimate desire.

When you wake, take note of why you were famous in your dream—did you get any indication? If you dreamed that people were taking notice of you, note in your dream journal what exactly they were noticing—was it your looks, your spending power, or that you were famous for a particular activity, such as your acting or musical talent or writing skill?

If you dream that you are surrounded by people clamoring for your attention, make a note of whether or not they seem happy to see you and are smiling. This could be a sign that you will have good fortune in the pursuit of your goals (see also *Faces*, page 62).

Also take note of where you are and what surrounds you in the dream—are you walking in rooms filled with expensive items? If a particular item strikes you, look up that item as a dream symbol; it may enrich your interpretation of your dream.

Sometimes dreams of fame can be prophetic, but traditionally such dreams are believed to indicate that you will suffer a downturn in your finances, relationships, or projects. Upon waking, itemize what may go wrong in your affairs and set up protective strategies to improve the stability of your projects. Do not rely on circumstances turning out in your favor.

A FREQUENTLY ASKED QUESTION

Why is it that when I fall in a dream, I wake up with a jerk, as though I really fell?

This usually just means that you have returned from dreaming to an awake state abruptly.

FAMOUS PEOPLE

SEE ALSO ROYALTY, PAGE 127.

If you imagine that a famous person knows you in a dream, it might indicate a subconscious desire for more recognition for your efforts. Such dreams usually mean that you will soon have the acknowledgment and recognition you crave. When you wake, make a list in your dream journal of all the things you feel you should be recognized for.

Dreaming of a particular famous person can be an indication that you will receive some help—from an unexpected outside source—in achieving your most desired goals.

Take note of any conversation that you had with the famous person—write down as much as you can remember, paying particular attention to whether or not he gave you any advice to help you achieve your goal.

It may be worthwhile to read up about the famous person if you don't know very much about him. This may help give you some idea as to why he appeared in your dream. The famous person may be an embodiment of what you want in your life, or there may be an aspect of his life that he dealt with in a way that appeals to you. Their presence in your dream could even be a warning not to go in the direction he chose.

If you dreamed of a particular actor or actress, you may be tapping into a particular archetype (see pages 170–171), a type of role that has a direct contact with the "collective unconscious."

A FREQUENTLY ASKED QUESTION

Are all my dreams always about me?

Not entirely. We may have some premonitory and visionary dreams that bear messages for other people. These types of dreams usually contain archetypal symbols and should be interpreted symbolically rather than literally. Alternatively, the person in the dream who is not yourself may be reflecting aspects of yourself—this may suggest that you have areas in your life that need attention.

Make a note of what role you last saw the actor or actress playing and try to understand what that particular role means to you. It could be that the character in the story resolved a problem in a way you may wish to emulate in your own life.

FATHERS

FOR **MOTHERS**, SEE PAGE 109.

The image of your father in your dream can represent a certain aspect of your life, depending on the nature of your relationship. If he was a strict parent, you may find that your father carries the traditional symbolic meanings of authority and duty. If he was not present when you were growing up or did not take an active role in rearing you, you may have evolved a different symbol for these characteristics.

In any dream scenario, images of your parents usually embody your feelings for them at that time. It is not uncommon to see parents fighting each other in a dream. This may reflect your worry that they are in conflict in reality. If you dream of being a father and you are not one already, this may be an indication that something unexpected will soon happen to you.

Seeing your father in your dream is thought to be a sign that your finances, career, or other activities involving duty and responsibility will improve. If your father has passed on, dreaming of him telling you something is believed to be an indication that you will receive some important news.

Generally, dreaming of scenarios that involve relatives is synonymous with learning interpersonal communication skills. Dreaming of individual family members usually means that you are resolving an issue with them during the dream state that you have failed to resolve in your wakened state.

Unpleasant dreams about your in-laws might reflect anxieties about incompatibility and lack of acceptance. If the dream is full of love and acceptance, you are feeling very comfortable with them. Dreaming about the parents of your friends is believed to be an indication that you will receive support and help from your friends.

FEARS

Fear of any kind in a dream is widely accepted as being a subconscious response to the unknown or unfamiliar in daily life, or to uncertainty about your future. Once the source of the fear is known, the dream emotion typically goes away.

Groups of people in a dream might represent fear that you are, or your property is, being taken for granted or used and abused.

A dream that the bed is shaking may reflect a fear that you will not wake at the correct time—your subconscious is attempting to stimulate you out of sleep. Such sensations may also indicate a return to the body after astral-traveling.

Feeling embarrassed in public is a similar indication of vulnerability, but also often suggests guilt about some wrongdoing of yours that is about to be revealed. Being accused of something usually indicates that you feel you are being judged unfairly. Perhaps people are pointing fingers in your dream—this can mean that you are feeling imposed upon, or that a situation has finally been resolved.

Feeling imposed upon (in your dream) suggests that you are not standing up for yourself in your everyday life; you may be being taken for granted or taken advantage of. A feeling of sacrifice might

also indicate bitterness, resentment, or anger aroused by lack of fulfillment, or by your belief that you must deny yourself to ensure another's prosperity or happiness.

Feelings of suspicion or the discovery of falsehood might be the subconscious stirring your conscious mind; look for deception in your waking life.

Dreaming of losing things might indicate a fear of not being able to hold onto something; perhaps you are not able to grasp a concept or you feel a relationship or career opportunity slipping away.

Images such as monumental landforms, prehistoric animals, impenetrable jungles, or vast deserts often suggest feelings of inadequacy and a belief that you are destined to fail.

FEET

A dream focused on feet indicates that you need to deal with any apprehension and uncertainty you feel about moving forward in your life. Walking barefoot in your dream may indicate that you will have to deal with some problems before you reach your goal. However, if you feel comfortable walking around in bare feet in your dream, and feel as if you are strongly connected to the ground, this could mean that you are putting an honest and straightforward effort into a particular project or aspect of your life.

Traditionally, dreaming of your feet feeling different sensations is believed to indicate the following meanings:

- broken feet—carelessness
- burning feet—jealousy
- cold feet—unhappy in love
- dirty feet—loss of reputation
- itchy feet—unexpected travel
- large feet—good health
- small feet—unnecessary anxiety
- sore feet—comfort in retirement.

FIGHTING

FOR DREAMS ABOUT PARENTS FIGHTING, SEE **FATHERS**, PAGE 65.

Any dream in which you are fighting with another person or you witness a fight is believed to be an indication of change. If you are one of those doing the fighting, take note of whom you are fighting—this may give you an idea about a change coming in your life. If you are fighting your boss in your dream, for instance, you may find that you get promoted or change jobs.

Traditionally, watching a fight is thought to be an indication that you have been wasting your time, being idle and unproductive when you really need to be changing some aspect of your life.

FIRE

Feeling hot or stifled in a dream suggests that you are physically too warm. Heat in a dream does not generally have other symbolic messages unless it also includes smoke or fire.

Generally, fire in a dream is a warning of trouble in some area of your life. Take note of what is burning and, if appropriate, how the fire started. This will give you a chance in real life to take precautions to prevent any trouble actually occurring.

Dreaming of a contained fire burning in a cozy fireplace is an indication of relaxation and feelings of contentment.

Flames, like ice, can be a symbol of ritual cleansing. However, fire around you can also suggest that you feel you are trying to find a solution to an out-of-control situation.

If the fire is emanating from you, it could suggest that you are going to be very successful at an activity you are about to try. Seeing a familiar person alive and well but surrounded by fire can also be a sign of imminent success and prosperity for you.

A dream in which you see a stranger in the background and fire in the foreground might reflect the efforts of a dead friend or relative to communicate with you.

Dreaming of a burning building often indicates helplessness and fear. Perhaps you believe you have gone too far or said too much and are unable to repair some damage that you have done to a relationship or situation. Your dream is giving you an opportunity to assess whether or not you can redress the situation in real life. It is nearly always worth a try.

Smoke generally indicates feelings of frustration and difficulty in expressing them.

FISH AND OTHER SEA CREATURES

In dreams, fish usually signify the awakening of your intuition and inspiration, the emergence of great ideas, and/or your enthusiasm and excitement about coming news and events. They might also signify future movement and change of direction in a situation that is currently beyond your control.

Traditionally, fish swimming in crystal-clear water is a symbol of wealth and a sense of abundance. A dream of a successful fishing trip, during which you have caught some fish, is believed to indicate the acquisition of knowledge. Catching a big fish is an omen of great success. Curiously, dead fish are believed to be an omen of an unexpected acquisition of money.

The dream image of a shark might occur when you fear that others may disregard you, or that you are incompetent. Traditionally, this is believed to be an omen of dishonesty from others or financial losses.

The whale is often a dream symbol of superior creativity, along with the freedom it demands and the freedom it brings. Dreaming of a whale is believed to indicate that you will be protected in your endeavors and released from your worries.

Dreaming of dolphins—enjoying the grace and freedom of their motion and the joyful sound of their laugh—is an indication that you will enjoy life and benefit from your work. Dolphins may also symbolize the intellect. They are renowned for their potential to communicate with humans. To dream of a dolphin might signify a period of fruitfulness in your life or a reinforcement of spiritual communication or direction.

A FREQUENTLY ASKED QUESTION

Do disaster dreams always precede disaster?

No—very few disaster dreams are premonitions. Most are manifestations of our subconscious mind as it connects to the universal awareness of the higher conscious mind. We are like radio receivers and senders, and we can often pick up information on many levels.

FLOODS

FOR **TIDAL WAVES**, SEE **OCEANS**, PAGE 114.

Unsurprisingly, dreams of a flood are an indication that you will have some obstacles to overcome in your real life. If the floodwater is clear, your obstacles may well be of short duration. The clear water may represent an emotion that overlays the issue confronting you but one that you will be able to curb, thus allowing you to get back on track fairly quickly. If the water is muddy, you will need to take a lot more time to sort through your emotional issues.

Being swept away by a flood may indicate that you are being swept off your feet by your unhappiness about a particular issue. Traditionally, being swept off your feet means that a person close to you is using you for his or her own advantage.

Take note of what the flood is covering—do you know? If the water is partly or fully covering the business district of a town, watch out for inappropriate emotional responses to money.

FLOORS

Working on a floor—tiling or laying timber boards, for instance— is traditionally an omen of good luck, particularly in business ventures, indicating that you have laid some solid groundwork that will pay off in the end.

If you are scrubbing or polishing the floor clean in your dream, it means you will be able to put the finishing touches on a particular project. If you are lounging or sitting on the floor, good luck will come your way.

FLOWERS

Flowers can be either a warning or an indication that you are feeling joyful and contented. Dreaming of bright, fresh flowers either still growing in the garden (also see *Gardens*, page 74) or attractively arranged in a vase symbolizes happiness and a delight in life.

If the flowers are wilting, dead, or messily arranged in stagnant water, there is a poor flow of energy in your life. Note in your dream journal where the cut flowers are placed in the room. Can you recognize the type of room? If it is a bedroom, you may be feeling unhappy about a relationship that is not meeting your expectations.

Traditionally, different types of flowers have specific dream associations. Seeing or smelling the flowers below may have the following dream meanings for you:

- carnations—the improvement of social status, prosperity, and happiness in the house or in your love life
- chrysanthemums—the acquisition of influential friends and the fulfillment of your hopes
- daffodils—happiness and longevity
- dahlias—financial success
- geraniums—the acquisition of wealth
- pansies—misunderstandings
- roses—social success and true love.

A dream of artificial flowers is generally symbolic of being undermined by deceit, jealousy, or betrayal. If you dream that you are visiting a florist, you may be about to embark on a long-term romance. If you notice in your dream that a flower is a particular color, also see *Colors*, pages 44–47.

FLYING

SEE ALSO **AIRCRAFT**, PAGE 26.

The sensation of flying, either in an aircraft or like a bird, represents either the freedom to advance without any limitation or the need to escape—perhaps for rest and recreation, to gain a different perspective, or to reassess your life.

Flying indicates that you are no longer stationary and are working toward changes in your life. Already, at a subconscious level, there is anticipation and excitement, and the celebration of a new sense of freedom. Such a dream might occur when you have achieved a goal you set for yourself, or met someone else's expectations. Flying may also represent a change of address or job, or settling into a quieter lifestyle. A flying dream might also indicate that you are having an out-of-body experience. Flying a kite in your dream—with the kite flying high—usually represents happiness and achievement.

FREEDOM

Images of freedom, or seeing yourself in the great outdoors or at a favorite location in a dream, usually indicate your ability to make choices, to be wherever you choose to be, and that a universe of opportunity and achievement awaits you. Flying is one of the strongest expressions of freedom (see above). Dreaming of running and feeling exhilarated, free, and happy suggests that you have finally been released from a great strain in your life, or that you have reached a level of accomplishment beyond your expectations.

FRIENDS AND FRIENDSHIP

If the dream involves feeling trust in something or someone, the subject of your dream may be a reality in your wakened state.

The dream image of a watcher at a distance might represent your feeling that someone is observing you in your waking state and monitoring your behavior or performance. An unknown person

standing near you in a dream usually represents someone you
would like to know. An unknown person talking to you often
represents the beginning of a new friendship.

When you dream that you and an unknown person are getting
to know someone new to you both, you might be uncertain about
how a new relationship in your waking life will develop.

An unknown person yelling at you generally represents someone
you are having problems getting to know and understand.

FURNITURE

Dreams of rooms crowded with furniture usually signify your
need to lighten your domestic load, or to simplify or tidy your
accommodation; a dream of a sparsely furnished environment
might occur when you are feeling unsupported, lacking in comfort,
or sorry for yourself.

A dream image of antique furniture may be a sign that you are
not up to date with current information or you are feeling out of
sync with your inner self or the rest of the world.

Different pieces of furniture have particular dream symbol
associations. A table is believed to represent an improvement in
different areas of your life, depending on what type of table you
have a dream about. If you dream of a dining table, for instance,
you may find yourself entertaining more and strengthening your
network of friends and mentors.

Dreaming of sitting in a comfortable chair or armchair can
mean that you are entering a time when you feel comfortable in life.
Traditionally, an empty chair symbolizes unexpected news.

A FREQUENTLY ASKED QUESTION
What does it mean when I fly in my dreams?

Flying dreams may indicate a creative and open phase in your life.
Many people report having flying dreams when they were
children, and then losing this as adults. This could mean a block in
openness and creativity. To some of us, flying could mean that
our lives are out of control.

G

GARDENS

SEE ALSO **FLOWERS**, PAGE 71, AND **HERBS**, PAGE 81.

Gardens are symbols of growth. In dreams, they represent self-identity and confidence. A flourishing garden often indicates a period of good fortune in your life and the fact that you are experiencing inner calm and happiness.

Blossoms usually represent creativity, being very happy with life, and looking forward to each day. If the garden does not have blooms, there may need to be a bit more zest in your life.

If part of the garden is dying, you may be feeling upset, depressed, or confused. A dream of plants with drooping leaves suggests that you are currently suffering mood swings and uncertainty.

Trees are widely accepted symbols of strength and determination. They often represent the changes of one's lifetime—from childhood through adolescence to adulthood—and the ability to see situations from different perspectives. Brightly colored trees usually signify creativity or change; richly colored trees usually signify spiritual awakening or self-discovery.

Bare trees usually mean that there is hard work ahead, and you can't see either the reasons for it or the results of it. Burned or scarred trees often indicate that you are feeling vulnerable or powerless.

Different trees can have different dream associations. For example:

- aspens—a period of loneliness
- crab apples—the flowering of new opportunities
- oaks—faithfulness in your relationship or marriage
- palm trees—material gain or a change in attitude that will enable growth
- pine trees—good health and longevity.

GATES

A gate swinging back and forth in a dream generally indicates something going out of your life and something coming in. A wide open gate often indicates acceptance of what is being offered to you and that there are going to be a lot more opportunities coming your way.

A closed gate signifies obstacles that are getting between you and your goals. However, if you dream that you are able to open the gate easily or that you can climb over it, you will be able to overcome any short-term difficulties you may be experiencing.

A locked and chained gate suggests that you are being stubborn and not allowing something or someone to come into your life. However, if you dream that you break the lock or knock the gate down, your frustration at not being able to proceed will be short-lived.

■ FOR **GEMS**, SEE **PRECIOUS AND SEMIPRECIOUS GEMS**, PAGE 121.

GHOSTS

Dreaming of a ghostly visitation can be quite unnerving. Seeing a ghost standing in front of you is traditionally believed to be quite a lucky omen. However, if the ghost is trying to communicate with you, it is possible that you are being given a warning.

In the couple of days after such a dream, reassess any proposals, projects, or investment prospects that you are uncertain about. Perhaps your gut feelings are against them or they are against your principles. You dream may be warning you not to take on the proposed activities and to rely on your first impressions despite being pressured by others.

Take note of whether you know the ghost—is it of your father or another male relative? If it is, heed his warning, particularly if you are facing some important financial decisions.

■ FOR **GLOVES**, SEE **CLOTHING**, PAGE 43.

GLASSES

Wearing glasses in a dream suggests an inability to see something properly in your waking life. However, if you usually wear glasses, the dream may suggest concern about your eyes.

GOSSIP

Hearing people gossiping about somebody else in a dream is likely to be a sign of your fear that people are secretly talking about you. Traditionally, if it is you being gossiped about, it is a contrary dream—it means you are going to hear good news in the near future.

Dreaming that you are caught gossiping about someone is believed to symbolize the start of family troubles and disagreements. It is important that in the couple of days after such a dream you make a conscious effort not to gossip about another person, no matter how innocuously, and to leave the room (without too much fuss) if your companions start gossiping.

GRADUATIONS

Dreams of graduating or witnessing a graduation ceremony are symbolic of change and the chance of rising in the world.

GRAVES OR GRAVEYARDS

SEE ALSO **BURIALS**, PAGE 39.

Seeing yourself walking through a graveyard in a dream might mean that you are reminiscing about a dead loved one or that you are feeling lonely and isolated. However, traditionally, standing at the grave of a friend during his or her funeral means that you will receive an inheritance; if you are attending the burial of a relative, you may be married soon.

Standing by a new grave surrounded by wilting flowers is symbolic of broken promises. The gravestone may provide you with information about who is giving the promise or what it is about.

GRIEF

Traditionally, dreams of grief, although uncomfortable, are believed to be contrary dreams—they are omens of joyfulness and happy tidings. If you have recurring dreams of loss and grief, try to take control of your grief dreams. Like all other dreams, they are there to help you.

There are two basic principles for dealing with dreams that are sad and unpleasant. One, record them in your dream journal, have a look at the symbols that emerge, and use lucid dreaming (see pages 176–179) to communicate with whoever is in the dream and ask them for clarity. Two, use your intuition to understand them, overcome the grief, and continue living your life.

Many people ask whether or not dreams of loss and grief can foretell a loss in our life. Generally this isn't the case—we often have this type of dream in order to release repressed emotions. If we don't allow ourselves to express emotions during our waking hours, they will come out symbolically in our dreams. In times of crisis, dreams can provide immeasurable comfort.

DREAM REPORT

Dealing with a grief dream

My husband had died two years earlier, and I was grief-stricken. I couldn't shake my grief—until I had the following dream:

I was watching a parade with many people marching down the street. They were all carrying candles. I knew I was looking for someone. Suddenly I saw my husband. He was smiling, and looked well and happy to see me, but his candle was not lit. This concerned me deeply. I found myself standing next to him. I was troubled that his candle was not lit. When I asked why, he told me that my tears kept putting the candlelight out.

I awoke to an amazing knowingness. I felt different and knew I wanted to let him go, to bless him, to thank him for the time we had had, and to release this sadness.

HAIR

A dream of a slick hairstyle suggests direction and purpose, whereas ruffled hair, perhaps hair that has been roughly cut, indicates lack of direction and uncertainty of purpose at the time of your dream.

Long, flowing locks usually signify high self-esteem; ill-kept hair illustrates the opposite. If your hair is looking in peak condition in your dream and you feel happy with how it looks, you are in good health.

If you dream that you are brushing your hair, you might be starting to take more notice of the way you present yourself to the world, how others see you and how you see yourself. It also indicates that you value others' opinions of you. Traditionally, combing or brushing someone else's hair is believed to indicate that a friend will soon require some help from you.

A dream in which you are losing your hair might be symbolic of feelings of helplessness, of an inability to resolve mounting difficulties in your life. However, if you have your hair cut, you will have success in your new ventures. Cutting someone else's hair is believed to indicate a degree of jealousy.

If you dream of other people brushing their own hair, you probably approve of them and feel comfortable with them. Traditionally, braiding your hair was believed to mean that you would be forging new friendships. However, if you dream that you were braiding someone else's hair, you are symbolically entwining yourself into an argument or disagreement with a friend. Take note of whose hair you are braiding. This may help you work out who it is you are having difficulties with.

HANDS

SEE ALSO **RINGS**, PAGE 125.

A dream of a hand in the dark usually signifies inner frustration and confusion. Open hands often mean that something is being revealed to you in its true form, and that you are now seeing clearly. Closed hands suggest that the reality of a situation is hidden from you, and that you need to be more assertive to gain access to the truth.

A dream of clapping hands indicates inner joy and excitement. Dreaming of hands that are waving or clapping at you represents endings, and the possibility of separations. Shaking hands in a dream symbolizes the renewal of a friendship or the mending of problems that have kept you and your friend apart.

Handcuffed hands might mean you are feeling curtailed by your own attitude or frame of mind, or by someone else's beliefs and expectations. Bandaged hands indicate the presence of short-term obstacles, and a broken hand is symbolic of carelessness in your affairs, which you need to rectify.

Clean hands indicate that you have completed or have yet to start an unpleasant task; dirty hands suggest that you feel compelled to do something that you don't want to do, perhaps because of peer pressure.

If you dream that you cannot see your hands, you might be worried that you cannot keep up with the demands of your busy life.

A dream that you have short fingernails suggests that you may have to make changes you are not happy about. If you have short fingernails and dream that you have long fingernails, there may be changes in your life in the near future.

A dream of fingers wearing rings, a symbol of opulence, might be an omen of good fortune, possibly a windfall.

■ FOR **HATS**, SEE **CLOTHING**, PAGE 43.

HEADS

Dreaming of suffering pain in the head is often a symbolic expression of stimulus and creativity. You are being urged to follow your creative path. Traditionally, experiencing pain in your head means that you must play your cards close to your chest and not be open about your own personal affairs for the moment. A blow to the head may represent overwork or too much tension.

Dreaming of a disembodied head indicates that you may need to consider solutions to your problems that involve your mind rather than your heart. A swollen head represents overconfidence—it is warning you to be humble in your success. Dreaming of having two heads may mean that you will soon get a promotion or another form of acknowledgment for your mental exertions.

HEARTS

Dreaming that you are suffering heartache is another contrary dream—it means that you may soon experience a joyful time. If you dream of heart-shaped objects, you may be feeling open to a new relationship.

HEIRLOOMS

Heirlooms are often dream symbols of your expectations or desires: items you wish to purchase, or goods and chattels of great significance or value to you.

DREAM FACT

Moving during your dreams

Your fingers, toes, and genitals will often move slightly when you dream, because all biological functions are active in this state. Only your eyes will move exactly as they do when you are awake.

HERBS

Herbs represent the subtleties of your personality and your innermost emotions. Dreaming of herbs growing in a garden usually symbolizes contentment and a sense of fulfillment. If you dream that your herbs are not growing well and in abundance, you may be facing the danger of losing your peaceful surroundings. You can reverse this possibility in real life by doing a meditation in which you visualize tending your herb garden—pulling out the weeds and tidying up the edges of the herb beds.

Many herbs and plants have particular dream associations. A four-leaf clover traditionally represents awareness and prosperity, for instance, and moss is often a symbol of creative or physical fertility.

If you smell herbs in your dream, or see yourself flavoring a dish with herbs, check the herbs listed below to see if their traditional dream associations have relevance to you:

- cloves—your worries will dissolve easily and without too much effort
- garlic—you will feel safe with this traditional herb of protection
- ginger—you may find yourself engaging in a torrid but short-lived romance
- lavender—you will experience harmonious relationships with friends and lovers (lavender is rarely used in cooking)
- rosemary—you will remember an important fact that will help you finally make a decision about something that has been concerning you for some time.

Be warned that dreaming about using hallucinogenic herbs and plants symbolizes a loss of self-esteem, and indicates that you may suffer from the actions of careless friends.

HOOKS

If you dream of hooks, you may fear being placed in a position where you will be forced to act against your feelings, and you may be concerned with how your peers will judge you.

HOUSES

It is often said that the space in which a person lives represents who they are. The more knowledge you have about a building in your dream, the more knowledge you are likely to have about yourself. If you are looking at a building's exterior in your dream and don't know what you will find inside, you are likely in the process of

uncovering something within yourself or in someone else, but have only gone just beyond the surface so far. An empty house or a strange environment might signify a soul-searching period of your life, or a change in your awareness that you are finding difficult to deal with.

Dreaming of constructing a building is often a sign that you are self-directed. If the building is a castle, your dream indicates that you are developing your individuality. If it is more like a fortress, you might need to develop a sense of protection—from yourself as well as from other sources. A mazelike building could indicate that you are caught in a confusing web of circumstances and you don't know the way out.

A dream about a small building might signify doubts about your present accommodation—perhaps you are being forced to leave and don't know where you will go. Alternatively, it might indicate career uncertainties. A large building suggests that the dreamer is excited about the future and is ready for new activities or more work.

If the building is tall, you might have a desire to be distinctive. On the other hand, the dream might be a subconscious suggestion that your potential is only just being tapped into. If the building is a home, it is usually a symbol of security and stability.

If the house is bright and cheery, you are likely to be feeling good about yourself. A dream image of a very clean house usually reflects being on top of life and ready for more challenges; dreaming of a dusty house usually indicates that you are overdue for a rest.

Dreams of damp and dank houses sometimes come to us when we are recovering from illness. A derelict house might be a subconscious expression of feeling left out or that no one cares about you.

When you dream of an overcrowded house, chances are you feel that someone or something is cramping your style, or people are encroaching on your living space—or perhaps your partner is taking up too much of the bed! A house filled with papers or books suggests that you are overloaded with work and unable to cope with the demands being placed on you.

Dreams about large and airy rooms are often symbols of your acceptance that you still have more to learn. Small, cramped rooms can feature in the dreams of busy people who would like to get out and enjoy themselves but have too many obligations to be able to do so.

Halls and corridors in a dream might indicate getting in touch with deep-seated fears, uncertainties, or problems. Stairs leading to nowhere suggest that you are feeling at a loss as to where life is taking you, that you are not getting what you want, or that a relationship is not progressing.

A dream of a rooftop suggests the release of restrictions and blocks. If you dream you are being watched from a rooftop, you may feel you are being evaluated.

A disturbing dream of neighbors might suggest festering problems with those who live nearby. A pleasant one might indicate neighborhood harmony.

DREAM TIP

Dreaming of the past

Dreaming about a particular period in history or people in period costume can represent a past life or your genealogical (ancestral) memory. Dreaming about a challenge or problem that occurred in another time or age may give you insight into an issue in your own life. Past-life dreams may seem strange in relation to your present life, but because they are played out as real situations and not symbols, you can usually understand whatever information is being presented.

ICE

Crystalline snow and ice are classic symbols of purity, clarity, inspiration, spirituality, and transformation—the cleansing of the body and the mind. Dreaming of an overwhelming amount of heavy snow or ice often symbolizes fear or apprehension.

There are a number of traditional meanings attached to ice and icicles; they depend on your interaction with them. If you slip and fall on ice in your dream you may well be about to face some obstacles. If you fall through the ice, it means that you may have broken through a barrier that has been keeping you from achieving your goals. Skating on ice connects with your work relationships; it may indicate that you will be acknowledged for your work, as you are very visible against the white of the ice. If you are joined by a partner while skating, the pressure on the ice increases—this kind of dream may indicate that you are involved in a dead-end relationship.

Seeing a snowscape in your dreams can indicate that you are sensing a complete change in your environment, and that your activities have slowed down. However, if you dream of sliding up and down icy hills, you may be relishing these changes and clearing obstacles from your path.

Snow on greenery may indicate that you will soon overcome delays and will succeed in your venture. If you notice icicles hanging from the eaves of a house, you may find that your anxieties will soon vanish. However, if the icicles are already starting to melt, you will need to conserve your money and be watchful of your investments.

IMPRISONMENT

To dream of prison might mean that you are feeling restricted by the differences in attitude between you and others in some area of your life. Dreaming that you are in prison, or that you can't escape from a particular room or part of a house, is a way of dealing with the frustrations you may be experiencing in the real world. Traditionally, this type of dream signifies that you are facing a number of obstacles to your goals.

Take note of any clues the dream may give you about why you are imprisoned and how you could escape. If you are plagued by recurring dreams of imprisonment, consider incorporating more movement in your everyday activities.

However, if you escape from prison in your dream, you will be able to overcome the obstacles and will succeed in your venture or project. If you constantly fail to find a way out, though, you may need help in the real world to overcome the obstacles facing you.

DREAM TIP

Emotions in our dreams

At all times, our mind is communicating with our body by means of our emotions, which are transmitted through our nervous system. While we are awake, how and what we think changes the way we respond. In our dreaming state, our emotions and feelings also influence our responses. When we dream, we experience real feelings and emotions, and they are just as strong as those felt when we are awake. If in our dreams we experience fear, anxiety, frustration, or pain, our bodies will produce the chemicals that correspond with those emotions just as if we were awake. For instance, sad images and thoughts will manufacture the chemicals associated with depression. Aggressive dreams will produce adrenaline, the "fight or flight" hormone.

INHERITANCES

Traditionally, it is believed that a dream of receiving an inheritance is more often than not a prophetic dream, and you will receive something—anything from a sum of 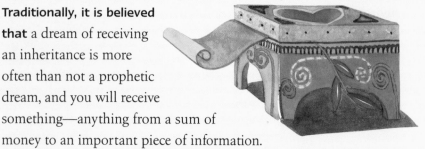 money to an important piece of information. This inheritance need not come from a relative; it can come from anyone who means you well. Accept your inheritance with gratitude and make sure you do not just put it aside. Use it—you are receiving this gift for a purpose. If you are not already aware of the gift's purpose, take note of any clues in your dream about what you should do with it.

■ FOR **INJURY**, SEE **ACCIDENTS**, PAGE 25.

INK

In the age of computers and laser printers, dreams of ink may well be becoming rare. Dreaming of spilling ink is a contrary dream—this action is symbolic of a positive outcome for a particular project or venture. The ink's being allowed to flow without restriction may be symbolic of freedom from restraint—there may have been something holding the project back from completion.

Curiously, dreaming of filling an inkpot with ink is an indication that you may soon be packing your bags to go on a journey.

INSANITY

Dreaming that you are insane is a contrary dream—it represents your release from a number of restrictions you have been facing; you will be in a position to hear good news. However, if you dream that another person in your dream is insane, you may receive an unhappy surprise from one of your friends.

INSECTS

In dreams, insects can represent petty issues that cause enormous irritation. Traditionally, they represent an obstacle you are facing that is small but annoying and requires resolution. Killing an insect in your dream indicates that your frustrations will not last for too long.

Large flying insects indicate that someone in your life has a problematic attitude and that you can't seem to be able to help them with this issue. Large, slow-moving insects suggest that you have overeaten or otherwise overindulged!

Dreams of small insects might represent your fastidiousness. Dreams where flies annoy you symbolize petty jealousies and backbiting. If you kill the flies, you will be able to sort out these problems.

Swarms of bees or ants might represent a fear of detail. Dreaming of bees has a number of traditional dream associations. The industriousness of bees is symbolic of great success in business. However, if you kill a bee, you may find that unreliable friends or associates will undermine your success, so take care in your waking life.

Dreaming of ants, particularly those building nests or hunting for food, might signify deep-seated anxiety or perfectionism. Alternatively, perhaps something will not be as you expect it.

Vibrantly colored moths and butterflies in your dreams traditionally signify prosperity and success. If their coloring is dark or lacking in distinction, your achievements might pass without recognition. Dreams of these insects might also indicate a loss of money or fear of a shortage of money. A white moth may be a warning to watch your spending. An iridescent moth usually represents lost or elusive opportunities, particularly for making money.

INSULTS

Dreaming that you are being insulted is believed to have a contrary meaning—it means you are well respected by your friends and colleagues. However, other traditional interpretations suggest that dreaming about giving or receiving insults is an indication of change. In particular, if a relative is being insulting to you, this may be a sign that you will soon change your home. If a person who is not your friend insults you in your dream, you may well be given the opportunity to change your job, even your career path.

INTOLERANCE

If you dream that you are being intolerant, this may be an omen of a rocky relationship with a friend. Note any clues in the dream as to why you feel intolerant. Do you feel your responses were justified in the dream? Do you feel that you flew off the handle without provocation? Ask yourself whether or not you have experienced any corresponding feelings in your waking life. If these have occurred in relation to a particular friend, try to work out better ways of resolving your feelings of intolerance. If someone is being intolerant to you in your dreams, you may soon receive a gift!

INTRIGUE

Experiencing some intrigue in your dream may indicate fear that you or someone else has not been discreet about your personal affairs. Note in your dream journal any clues your dream gives you about how to rectify the situation. You may need to do some damage control in your waking life.

INVENTIONS

Dreaming that you are inventing something new or working on an invention is an indication that you are using your skills creatively and profitably. This dream tells you that you will achieve and even surpass your goals.

INVISIBILITY

SEE ALSO **OUT-OF-BODY DREAMS**, PAGE 115.

If you experience the sensation of invisibility in a dream, perhaps you are not letting yourself see things as they really are in your life. Or perhaps you are playing out a desire to spy on somebody to discover his or her hidden motives. That you have been invisible in your dream may also indicate that you are going to experience a change in your life or circumstances, so prepare yourself. Your dream will give you clues as to why you need to be invisible.

INVITATIONS

Traditionally, dreaming of receiving a written invitation is an indication that you can anticipate some additional expenses. Invitation dreams are often contrary dreams, representing a downturn in social or other types of activity around you, and possibly leaving you with a feeling of unhappiness and loneliness. The written invitation may indicate that there is distance between you and the real world of friends. However, if the invitation is verbal, you will engage more fully with your friends.

DREAM HISTORY

The early days

Recognition of the importance of dreams goes back thousands of years. The interpretation of dreams has played a major role in virtually every society that has ever existed. Tribal high priests, medicine men, or shamans often used dreams to foretell the fortunes and direct the travels of nomadic tribes. Egyptian papyrus documents dating back to 2000 B.C. discuss dreams and their interpretations.

JARS

Empty jars in a dream generally indicate that you are in the process of acquiring a specific skill; while a dream of full jars indicates that you have achieved competency or proficiency in a particular area.

Traditionally, an empty jar suggests that there is something missing in your life. Note in your dream journal any clues that help you work out what area of your life might be deficient.

JEWELRY

Precious jewelry in a dream often signifies good fortune and prosperity. Tarnished jewelry generally signifies fears or uncertainties about money, and fake jewelry is an indication of vanity and blindness to the reality of a situation.

DREAM TIP

Responding to your dreams promptly

If there are issues that you continue to ignore consciously, there will eventually be a subconscious eruption of some magnitude to get your attention. Your dreams may become more explicit, more exaggerated, more bizarre—and perhaps even terrifying—until you respond positively to the knowledge they offer you. Sometimes a simple conscious acknowledgment of a problem will allow the subconscious to begin work on producing a positive outcome.

Dreaming that you are giving jewelry is an omen of good fortune—your generous nature will reap you rewards. However, if jewelry is stolen in your dream, take some precautions against loss of money or troubles in business negotiations.

Assess what it is about the jewelry that strikes you in the dream. Consider whether it is that the piece of jewelry is:

- a particular type of accessory, such as a necklace, bracelet, earrings, or rings (for *Rings*, see page 125);
- made from a particular precious metal, such as gold, silver, or copper (for *Metals*, see pages 104–105);
- set with pearls or a particular precious or semiprecious gem (for *Pearls*, see page 118; for *Precious and Semiprecious Gems*, see page 121).

Seeing this particular type of jewelry could be the result of a combination of things. The piece of jewelry could be something that is given to you by a friend or lover for a particular purpose, or something that is actually an inheritance (see page 86) or an heirloom (see page 80), for example. Also, try to remember the color of the gem that was set in the piece of jewelry (see pages 44–47).

Wearing an attractive necklace or pendant in your dream is a symbol of success in love; wearing a bracelet is indicative of success in love and in business. Earrings indicate that you should improve your listening skills.

DREAM TIP

The flow of information during dreaming

Information moves from the unconscious to the higher conscious mind and vice versa. It rarely flows from the conscious mind to the higher conscious mind. Keeping these three levels of thought in communication with each other and in harmony is essential for a balanced life.

JOY

Feelings of joy in a dream are an indication of the development of harmony and balance in your family situation. However, if you are feeling joyful in your dream because someone who was giving you problems has fallen, or is now sick or dying, your behavior and actions will be called into question.

If you do feel a vindictive sense of joy in your dreams, take note in your dream journal of any clues or warnings about how to lessen such unworthy feelings; they may indicate a misplaced sense of insecurity and inferiority.

JUDGES

SEE ALSO **TRIALS**, PAGE 148.

Dreaming that you are a judge suggests that you are required in your waking life to make some hard decisions. Do not make any hasty decisions—your dream is warning you to take into account all sides of a situation and to make a judgment fairly and impartially. If you do this in your waking life, you may find that most problems or obstacles will be of short duration.

JUGGLERS

Dreaming that you are a juggler symbolizes the fact that you may be juggling too many bits of information or trying to handle too many tasks, and this is making it difficult for you to settle or focus on any one particular path.

Traditionally, dreaming of a juggler means that you may soon be offered an unexpected opportunity, an opportunity that seems too good to be true. If this does happen, the dream is an indication that you should take the opportunity, regardless of the fact that you have some doubts about it.

JUNGLES

Traditionally, a jungle is considered a bad omen in terms of a romantic fling or business: it indicates that if you do not take heed, you may become involved in a foolish and time-wasting romance or an unfortunate business venture involving a friend.

As a jungle is a symbol of strong, primal growth, it is important not to squander this energy on matters that are unworthy. Seek relationships with people you can honor and respect, and work with experienced business associates whom you trust.

For some people, the jungle is a fearful place: it can symbolize deep commitment or an environment where only the strongest survive. Note in your dream journal your reaction to the jungle, and whether or not there are some fears or a lack of confidence that you need to face.

JUNK

Dreams about junk often indicate neglect of important matters that should be addressed. Such a dream might occur when you need to act positively to counter the negative effects of lack of enthusiasm.

If you dream that you are surrounded by junk, you may need to clear out the clutter in your home and workplace, heeding the

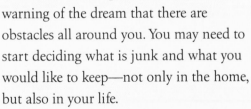

warning of the dream that there are obstacles all around you. You may need to start deciding what is junk and what you would like to keep—not only in the home, but also in your life.

K

■ FOR **KEYS**, SEE **LOCKS**, PAGE 99.

■ FOR **KILLING**, SEE **CRIMES**, PAGE 48.

KISSES

The meanings of kisses in dreams vary as much as they do in the waking world, but they are usually good omens of love, respect, and friendship. A dream kiss could also mean that you are ignoring, or even dismissing, something you feel is of little consequence in your daily life.

A kiss from a friend or relative indicates that your affection for them is reciprocated; dreaming of a kiss from a parent often means

you have an unfulfilled need to feel nurtured. Kissing a baby or child, on the other hand, whether it is someone you know or a stranger, indicates your need to give love and support.

A more passionate lover's kiss often represents a deepening phase in your relationship. Dreaming of a very emotionally charged kiss may also suggest that you need to work on being more open in your waking life to embraces and nurturing from your loved one.

Kissing someone you admire, whether that person is someone you see regularly or a celebrity you have never met, is—sadly—not usually prophetic; it often indicates that you are seeking to develop in yourself some aspect of that person's nature.

Passionate kisses from strangers warn against the emotional hazards of brief, superficial relationships. Unwelcome kisses of this nature show your need to establish personal boundaries—physical or psychological—and kisses from anyone you find extremely unattractive are a warning that suppressed emotions or situations from your past are coming back to haunt you.

Blowing someone a kiss can be a sign that your love or friendship for that person is cooling, or that you are soon to be parted. A kiss on the forehead, especially from a respected older person, indicates that you are being given a blessing to follow a certain path.

■ FOR **KITES**, SEE **FLYING**, PAGE 72.

KNIVES

Knives in dreams frequently indicate present or future dangers or confrontations. A particularly sharp knife or a scalpel suggests that there are aspects of your life that need to be cut away, such as a childhood trauma, an addiction, or an unhealthy relationship. A sharp knife in a nonthreatening situation symbolizes your need to make a very critical decision.

Knives, like the swords in Tarot cards, often represent the intellect, so the sharper the knife, the sharper the wit. If you are in possession of a sharp-edged blade in your dream, you need to give your own intellect more respect. If someone else is holding the blade, you may be feeling intellectually outclassed in some situation.

A blunt knife, on the other hand, embodies dull thinking, unproductive work, or the need to exert a great deal of energy for small gains. A rusty knife suggests an issue that has become dangerous through neglect.

A knife in the hands of a stalker or attacker often means that you are empowering your fears. The person with the knife is your own creation, since you are the dreamer, so it is within your power to disarm that person with a mere thought. Similarly, we can often disarm our fears by the force of our will.

A thrown knife represents an issue that you are unable to stop, but which will be resolved for better or worse in the very near future. It may also represent your fear of gossip or of not fitting in with a group.

Different types of knives have particular meanings: a pocketknife represents your resourcefulness and practicality; a switchblade, a volatile temper; a dagger, an unforgiving nature; a stiletto, premeditated cruelty and cunning; and a machete, the need to clear obstacles in your path.

Table knives generally indicate hospitality, and unusually fine silverware suggests an improvement in your standard of living.

L

LADDERS

There are a number of points to note in your dream journal about any dream concerning a ladder. First, were you climbing the ladder? Having difficulty climbing a ladder often indicates that you are exceeding your natural limitations; climbing easily indicates achievement and personal direction.

As with elevators (page 60), if you are climbing up the ladder you are aiming to achieve a goal. Climbing down a ladder suggests that you are retreating from your goals or that you have experienced some form of disappointment. However, you could also be returning to the ground to strengthen your resolve or gather information that you need to achieve your ambitions. You may be seeking a firmer foundation. Climbing down a ladder in a dream, particularly if it feels rickety or unstable, may be also an indication that you are taking care of details that could otherwise prevent you from succeeding in your goal. Quickly climbing down a ladder in the face of some form of danger is a good omen—it means you are able to successfully escape some serious problems.

If you dream of feeling dizzy while being up a ladder, you have overreached your goals for the moment and need to rethink your plan of action. Climbing an extremely tall ladder indicates that you will reach your ambitions; your returns will be more modest if you have climbed only a small or a medium-height ladder (with a dozen or so rungs).

According to superstition, walking under a ladder attracts bad luck. Dreaming of walking under a ladder is believed to be an omen of good luck. Dreams of accidents with a ladder generally indicate that you are going to have to contend with obstacles in your path or with disharmony in your family. If you fall from a ladder, you may soon be involved in a quarrel with family or friends.

If you dream that you are walking around carrying a ladder, you should expect to be asked for some advice or financial aid by a friend.

LAMPS

If your dream features a lighted lamp, you will achieve success and your achievements will be recognized and honored. To understand what area such wonderful fulfillment will occur in, make a note in your dream journal of what the lamp is standing on, if it is a table lamp, and what type of room it is in.

For dream associations of different types of tables, see *Furniture*, page 73. If your lamp was standing on a study desk, for instance, you will succeed in your intellectual pursuits. If the lamp is standing in the kitchen, perhaps the potential of your cooking skills will be fully realized!

If the light of the lamp is red, this is a warning signal. Traditionally, red light is an indication of passion and intense emotions, such as anger. Look at *Colors*, pages 44–47, if the light of your lamp is another color.

Traditionally, the lamp not being lit is a sign of disappointment. However, if you are the one who turns out the lamp in the dream, you may be indicating that you wish to finish working or doing your usual activities and have a break.

LAUGHTER

Laughter, friendly or joyous, usually signifies excitement or harmony, but traditionally, hearing laughter in dreams has a contrary meaning: if you are laughing, it is a warning of impending troubles and disappointments. If you hear someone else laughing, unless it is a child, you may suffer through an unhappy friendship. Only children's laughter is believed to be an omen of good luck. Outbursts of harsh or raucous laughter in your dream might indicate that someone is mocking you.

■ FOR **LAVATORIES**, SEE **TOILETS**, PAGE 144.

■ FOR **LAVENDER**, SEE **HERBS**, PAGE 81.

LETTERS

Receiving letters in your dreams means that prosperous change may be imminent. However, dream associations vary, depending on what type of mail you receive. If you receive a love letter or a letter that gives you some good news, such as that you have passed an examination with flying colors or that you have won some money, it means that your life in the immediate future will be successful.

Letters that contain bad news are not contrary dreams: they indicate that you will be struggling to achieve your goals.

A dream of outgoing mail might indicate a concern with bills you have to pay. However, traditionally, sending a letter in your dream represents receiving joyful tidings. Dreams where you are writing a love letter indicate that you have some regrets about a dead-end romance.

There are a number of dream associations concerning the mishandling of letters. If you read someone else's mail, deliberately

invading their privacy, you may feel that your own privacy is being invaded—you will need to set some boundaries for yourself in your waking life.

Dreaming that you are ripping up a letter is thought to symbolize a loss of money; hiding a letter is an indication that a particular friend or lover is unfaithful.

An empty mailbox usually indicates that you are waiting for something or waiting to hear from someone. An overflowing mailbox, or one drenched by rain, often represents your fear that you will not hear from a loved one.

You will usually receive money after a dream of a red mailbox. A white mailbox might reflect a feeling of being lost. Frequently, dreaming of a mailbox is a way for the subconscious to get you in touch with memories and fears and clear them out.

LOCKS

SEE ALSO **DOORS**, PAGE 56, AND **GATES**, PAGE 75.

Coming across anything locked is an indication that you are dealing with some strong opposition to a particular plan or pathway. If you see past a locked gate, you will still have an opportunity to jump the gate or fence and get back on track with your goals. The obstacles are not insurmountable.

However, if you can't see beyond a locked door, you may need to be creative about how to get beyond any barriers in your life or reassess whether or not you should be going on a particular path.

Traditionally, a padlock barring the way is an indication that you may be up against some serious legal or financial predicaments if you continue toward a particular goal. Note in your dream journal any clues as to what particular project or direction will lead you into such problems. If you can remember to do it, it is worthwhile to make a note of the last thing you were thinking of at night—if you were worried or anxious about a particular issue.

The padlock dream associations can be mitigated if you find a key to the lock in your dream. Keys are powerful dream symbols— if you do find a key you will find a solution to the obstacles blocking your way. If you are actually given a key, you will not be alone in finding a solution but will have a mentor helping you.

Breaking the key in the lock may mean that an opportunity has passed you by, or that it did not pan out the way you had hoped it would. Traditionally, broken and lost keys are believed to indicate disappointments, arguments with friends, or an unfulfilled love life.

LONELINESS

Dreaming that you are lonely and without a friend in the world is traditionally a contrary dream—it means you will find yourself invited to various social gatherings.

Check whether or not this actually occurs by keeping a journal of your waking life (even a brief one) as well as your dream journal.

If it does not, your dreams of loneliness may indicate the frustration of not being able to connect with the people around you. For instance, you may be walking in a crowd of people but somehow you do not touch anyone and all the people passing you seem to be looking right through you.

Recognizing anyone else in your dream of loneliness could be an indication that it will be of benefit if you reconnect or improve the

quality of connection with that person, if possible. Even if that person is no longer alive, you can make a gesture in her memory, such as lighting a candle or getting out her picture and placing it in a position of honor, on your mantelpiece or desk, for example.

LOSSES OR BEING LOST

If you dream that you have lost something, you may encounter some obstacles caused by forgetting to do something or take care of a particular detail. However, if you find the object, your frustration will only be temporary.

Dreams about being lost often symbolize confusion and a sense of being misunderstood. They may be full of feelings of uncertainty and apprehension. By paying attention to where you are lost (such as in a school, a house, or a garden), you may gain a sense of which areas of your life you need help in.

LOVE

SEE ALSO **KISSES,** PAGE 94, **MARRIAGES,** PAGE 102, AND **WEDDINGS,** PAGE 160.

Feeling unconditional love in a dream is an indication that you have a high level of support from your lover, family, and friends.

If you do not feel this in your waking life, make a note in your dream journal and think about whether or not you have been withdrawn lately and have not appreciated the support and love of the people around you.

Generally, love in a dream suggests harmony and pleasure in life; it is the dream of someone who is content with his or her present life and enthusiastic about the future.

A dream of love might also be the prelude to an increased sense of creativity and inspiration, or to the feeling of great personal satisfaction that comes with the successful completion of a major task.

Depending on your personal circumstances, it might also mean the beginning of a relationship with that dream lover you've been searching for. However, dreaming of a love tainted by deceit and lies, such as having an affair behind your partner's back, is usually an indication that you will suffer losses through your ill-considered actions.

If you dream of lovers, it's likely that you want to attract someone into your life or someone is trying to attract you into their life. It might even mean you are meeting someone on the astral plane, someone who would like to come into your life during an out-of-body experience. Traditionally, watching lovers is believed to augur well for your business ventures; it may be symbolic of a happy, satisfying partnership.

MARRIAGES

SEE ALSO **ENGAGEMENTS**, PAGE 61.

Dreams of a marriage ceremony naturally
concern partnerships—the nature of the
participants, setting, mood, and so on gives us
clues as to what particular form of union is
being brought to our attention. If you are single but romantically
attached, a dream marriage involving someone you love and adore
is a sign that you are ready to make a commitment that will bring
about growth and success.

The dream may be very literal, suggesting that you are indeed
ready to marry the person in question, or it may be symbolic, with
the marriage representing a different type of partnership, such as a
business relationship, which has the potential to be harmonious.
The key to deciding whether the dream is symbolic or not is the
emotion associated with the wedding (see *Weddings,* page 160).

If you are single and don't currently have anyone special in your
life, the dream of a marriage will often signify your readiness to
form a new and lasting relationship. However, if you dream of
marriage to a stranger, it is likely that you are nervous about
commitment, about getting involved at all. If you dream that you
are marrying someone who is familiar but who appears different in
the dream, it could be that you fear the consequences of this
relationship changing for the worse.

If you are already married and dream of marrying your spouse,
you may feel the need to reenergize the relationship. If you dream of
marrying someone different, your current marriage may indeed be
in trouble! But once again, check the emotional content of the
dream. The marriage in the dream may well represent an entirely
different form of partnership.

If you dream that someone else is marrying the person you
desire, it could mean that you are holding on to old loves.

■ FOR **MAZES**, SEE **PARKS**, PAGE 117.

MEDICAL MATTERS

SEE ALSO **DISEASES**, PAGE 54.

Dreams involving medical practitioners and procedures are usually clear indications of areas of your life that need to be changed. How you feel about medical issues in your waking life will greatly influence how you interpret the dream equivalents. To some, medical procedures of various sorts are very frightening. Others are much less troubled by such fears and view the medical profession as purely beneficial.

A dream of a medical examination often indicates your awareness of a problem you have not allowed to surface; a dream of a doctor's waiting room suggests that you feel unable to make the first move toward solving a problem.

Depending on their context in a dream, hospitals may evoke either your fears or your sense of being nurtured. However, whether they are associated with negative or positive emotions, they represent your need to have some aspect of your life healed, even if this process requires you to take time out of your everyday life.

The nature of the medical procedure taking place in the hospital or elsewhere gives an indication of the problem being considered by your dreaming self. For example: surgery indicates that a problem you have kept hidden for some time is being addressed; back treatment may suggest that you feel unsupported; and the plastering of a broken limb indicates a feeling of restriction in some area of your life.

To dream of ambulances and emergency treatments shows that you can no longer delay changing matters for the better; a dream of swallowing medicine indicates that you are already taking steps to heal troubled areas of your life.

If a loved one is the subject of the medical treatments in your dream, it may indicate that you feel you have been neglecting them.

METALS

SEE ALSO **MOON**, PAGE 108.

Metals, like gemstones, plants, and many other naturally
occurring substances, have a long history of symbolic associations.
These associations are, according to some theorists, stored in the
collective unconscious of the human race and are accessible to our
dreaming selves even if we do not consciously know of them.
Whether this is true or not, many metals seem to have evoked
similar responses from people in widely differing cultures.

These correspondences continue to be added to as we find new
purposes for various metals. For instance, it is only relatively
recently in human history that lead has become associated with
both bullets and poisoning.

ALUMINUM

Because of its lightness, aluminum items in a dream represent
matters that look more important than they actually are.

BRASS

Brass, which is often used in decoration as a substitute for gold, can
often symbolize a grand show not backed up by substance.
Alternatively, through its association with money and musical
instruments, it can suggest cheerful celebration.

COPPER

Long associated in alchemy with the planet Venus and the goddess
of that name, copper is associated with love, harmony, and good
fortune. Copper items in a dream often evoke a
gentle, loving atmosphere.

GOLD

Gold, as you would expect, symbolizes wealth,
success, and power, but a dream overly decorated with this metal
suggests ostentation. Dreams about panning or digging for gold
suggest fruitless get-rich-quick schemes. Simply happening upon
gold, however, means unexpected good luck is around the corner.

IRON

Long used in weapons and armor, iron symbolizes protection or a
preparedness to fight for your beliefs. Rusty iron, however, suggests
that you have endangered yourself through neglect.

LEAD

The heaviness of this metal suggests weighty matters; the presence
of leaden objects in a dream indicates oppressive situations.

SILVER

Silver is traditionally associated with not only wealth but also the moon, which in turn relates to psychic powers, changing fortunes and enchantment. Its presence in a dream can hint that there is a prophetic message to be found.

MIRRORS

Dreams in which you see yourself reflected in a mirror signify how you perceive your inner nature. If the reflection seems pleasing, or at worst neutral, you are on fairly safe ground, but if the image is distorted or somehow displeasing, you may have a degree of shame or guilt about some issue. Similarly, if the mirror itself is dirty, cracked, or partly hidden, there are issues you are hiding from yourself that need to be faced.

A broken mirror may occur in a dream when others are questioning your beliefs or you are comparing their beliefs with your own. It might also indicate the shattering of an illusion or an imminent illness or injury. Seeing your own reflection in a broken mirror indicates that you are struggling to come to terms with feelings of grief or loss.

Seeing yourself in a large or very ornate mirror often predicts a significant success in an important project or a major change for the better in how you are perceived by others.

A dreamer who looks into a mirror only to see someone else's face reflected may be feeling controlled by another person, particularly if the other face is familiar. Alternatively, the other face may represent a quality in the dreamer that he or she has been suppressing. Seeing several other people in a mirror, as if through a window, suggests a wistful, hopeful, or perhaps nostalgic state of mind. On the other hand, if you find the view through a window obscured by your own reflection, personal issues are getting in the way of seeing the world as it really is.

Hand mirrors may indicate narcissism, especially if the mirror is particularly ornate or even bejeweled. Unusually small mirrors, or mirrors concealed beneath a covering of some sort, signal a reluctance to examine your motives.

MONEY

SEE ALSO **COINS**, PAGE 44.

Where financial matters occur in dreams, they frequently relate to broader issues of well-being, happiness, and self-worth.

Dreaming of gaining a substantial amount of money often has less to do with actual wealth than with a desire to be seen as successful. If the money is gained through your own efforts, the dream indicates a sense of confidence that such a thing is attainable. If, on the other hand, the money is won, found, or inherited, that sense of self-confidence may be lacking, which will make the likelihood of improving your financial situation much harder.

Loss of money in a dream is no more likely to be reflected in waking life than winning it is. It generally only reflects your fears, just as winning money reflects hopes. A dream of financial loss through carelessness shows that you are aware of your tendency to overlook details; loss through misfortune may be a warning against taking certain matters for granted; and loss through theft often indicates that you feel unworthy of good fortune and that the universe would be justified in taking it away from you without a moment's notice.

While dreams of finding money rarely come true, a dream in which you locate a sum of money in your own home suggests that you have an untapped talent waiting to be brought out. If you see

yourself involved in gaining money dishonestly, through theft or embezzlement, you may either lack confidence in being able to improve your finances through any less desperate means, or you may simply have a hidden desire to break some rules and lead a more dramatic life.

MONSTERS

Dream monsters come in all shapes and sizes; they frequently represent our fear of the unknown, the future, or repressed emotion. Being pursued by such a creature in a dream often means that you are in an equally unpleasant phase in your waking life—your stress levels have built up to the point where not even sleep reduces them.

Anxieties about health, finances, relationships, professional lives, and so on produce in your body the same feelings the earliest humans had when faced with pursuit by some long-toothed, sharp-clawed carnivore. This fear of predators is so deeply ingrained into our subconscious that sleep often sets variants of these beasties loose in our dreams. Dream monsters are as much individuals as we are, but certain subspecies tend to represent similar issues to most of us.

ANIMAL MONSTERS

Many monsters—of various sizes—look like insects, reptiles, rats, and other creatures. Many people have phobias about certain creatures, so their stress-created pursuers naturally take on that most feared form. For those without such phobias, biological monsters can embody more specific fears. Insect-inspired monsters, for instance, whether huge or just numerous, often represent situations that should have been insignificant but have grown unduly large. Animal monsters can also represent your fear—unreasonable or valid—of a particular disease.

ANIMATED DEAD PEOPLE

Zombies, stalking skeletons, ghosts, and the like often represent matters that you had thought were settled, but which refuse to stay put in their unquiet grave.

PEOPLE TURNING INTO MONSTERS

People turning into monsters can often cause the most frightening of nightmares, since they begin as people we love before morphing into something monstrous. You need to consider whether the person in question really does have a dark side, or if it is merely a fear in your mind.

VAMPIRES

Whether they are attractive or hideous, vampirish figures represent people or issues that habitually drain your energy or resources.

WEREWOLVES

Humans who take on animal form in a dream represent your aversion to some primal aspect of your own nature, most frequently anger or sexuality. You may need to explore these areas and befriend the internal beast.

MOON

From the earliest times, the moon's effect on both the tides and the menstrual cycle has been observed. It has led to associations with other mysterious flows of energy, such as psychic and magical powers, romantic love, artistic inspiration, and dreams themselves.

The shifting phases of the moon represent harmonious change. Dreaming of a full moon often indicates that you will enjoy a flash of inspiration, achieve success (especially in romantic or creative ventures), or enjoy increased wealth, perhaps through an inheritance. For a woman, it may be a sign of ovulation or of an undetected or future pregnancy.

A crescent or gibbous moon represents beginnings and endings, depending on whether it is waxing or waning (many people can't consciously differentiate one from the other, but that's the sort of detail the subconscious is good at noticing—you should always pay close attention to the shape of the moon in a dream and check the real moon's phase when you wake).

If the moon is hidden by clouds or perhaps even eclipsed in your dream, inspiration and good fortune may be in short supply for a while, but as the moon is the mistress of change, the situation will not be permanent.

A dreamed glimpse of the moon through a window suggests that you are being invited to explore the mystical side of life. A dream of walking, dancing, or bathing by moonlight indicates that you are in a period of your life that is enchanted in the best possible way; being naked by moonlight shows an unusually strong psychic receptivity. To see your shadows cast by moonlight indicates your

deepening awareness of the subtle tides ruling your life.

To dream of actually traveling to the moon, whether by spacecraft, broomstick, or any other form of locomotion, shows an inner assurance that nothing is impossible for you.

MOTHERS

SEE ALSO **FATHERS**, PAGE 65.

Everyone's relationship with their mother is utterly unique; yours will set the tone for every dream you have on the subject. Likewise, every mother will have her own very distinct feelings about motherhood. There are, however, some constants in dreams about motherhood.

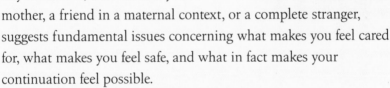

Since we experience our first inklings of ourselves while still in the womb, one of our most fundamental emotions around the idea of motherhood involves our need for nurture. The appearance of a mother in your dream, whether it is your own mother, a friend in a maternal context, or a complete stranger, suggests fundamental issues concerning what makes you feel cared for, what makes you feel safe, and what in fact makes your continuation feel possible.

As we grow older our needs change enormously, but maternal imagery in a dream may be a signal that we need to focus on what those fundamental needs are right at this moment, and prioritize them.

Women especially, whether they have given birth or not, may need to examine secondary considerations after dreams of motherhood, particularly regarding how they nurture others. One of the major forms of nurture we require from our parents is approval, so dreams of motherhood will often involve that aspect more strongly than any other.

Maternity may also symbolize creativity of all kinds. A dream of someone heavily pregnant or giving birth may mean that your current projects, whether artistic, commercial, or domestic, will blossom.

MOUNTAINS

Mountains in dreams usually represent your aspirations, particularly when you are either climbing or you discover that the path ahead is about to rise steeply. Just as craggy, imposing mountains have more grandeur than small hills, so the more challenging projects you undertake have the potential to become your major achievements in life.

The appearance of mountains in your dream will often indicate how you are feeling about your current goals. If the mountain can be scaled fairly easily, you may feel insufficiently challenged. Alternatively, if you are faced with a snow-covered peak of Himalayan proportions in your dream, you may have set your sights too high.

Remember, a mountain doesn't necessarily need to be conquered—the true goal may lie beyond the obstacle. You don't have to climb a mountain just because it is there!

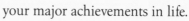 FOR **MURDERS**, SEE **CRIMES**, PAGE 48.

MUSEUMS

A dream of a museum frequently indicates your need to revisit aspects of your past in order to make informed decisions about the future.

Sadly, museums are often considered stuffy, lifeless collections of dead creatures and relics of dead cultures, and this may be reflected in a dreamed museum, along with a feeling that the past has nothing to teach you. However, if you remember focusing on an exhibit in your dream, you may need to do something similar in your waking life.

If you dream of a dull-seeming museum, you may need to focus on your past in order to find a solution to a problem in your current life, or to bring back some magic into your life.

MUSIC

SEE ALSO **SOUNDS**, PAGE 136.

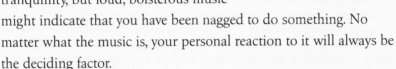

Music of all sorts may be encountered in dreams; its meaning will be determined by the degree to which the dreamer enjoys it. Soft, gentle music usually symbolizes peace, comfort, and tranquillity, but loud, boisterous music might indicate that you have been nagged to do something. No matter what the music is, your personal reaction to it will always be the deciding factor.

A particular piece or style of music will often evoke memories—you may be looking back nostalgically or the memories may hold answers to issues currently troubling you.

Songs, familiar or otherwise, often express the message of a dream. Try to remember the lyrics if the words are clear. At the simplest level, a particular love song may express an aspect of your romantic life that you haven't considered.

In other dreams, the song lyrics may contain subtler hints about how to resolve waking concerns. For example, a song as simple as "Happy Birthday" might have nothing to do with your birthday or that of a friend or relative, but may predict a pregnancy and the arrival of a healthy addition to the family.

Ethnic music of various sorts may suggest the need for travel, perhaps to the region of the music's origin or perhaps merely to exotic locations. Hymns may suggest either spiritual growth or the precise opposite, depending on what feelings you have about this type of music.

Loud orchestral music or opera may signify a tendency to overdramatize situations; quiet tunes picked out on a single instrument often suggest a need for meditation. Composers and songwriters often receive melodies or lyrics in their dreams, as their subconscious works in conjunction with their conscious desire to create music. One of the most frequently recorded songs of all time, the Beatles' "Yesterday," is a prime example of this.

N

NAKEDNESS

When you see yourself without clothes in a dream, your subconscious is probably reflecting your fear of being vulnerable or feeling exposed. Take note in your dream journal about where you see yourself being naked.

If you are naked in a safe place, you may need to work on feeling comfortable with how you feel inside as opposed to how you feel about your appearance. If you are naked and looking at yourself in the mirror, you may be trying to reconnect with and accept yourself.

Dreaming that you are naked in a public area and your nakedness is not being commented on could symbolize the fact that you are not as vulnerable as you think you are. Make a note in your dream journal about how people reacted to you when you were naked, if you can remember.

However, if you are ostracized for your nakedness in your dream, make a note about who is commenting on your state. If it is someone you know, you may have uncovered the fact that someone is making you feel vulnerable in your waking life and that you will need to address this situation. Perhaps you need to decide—or

realize—that that person's opinion of you should not affect you at all.

Traditionally, nakedness is associated with being without material possessions. Dreaming of being naked is a contrary dream, indicating that you will soon acquire money, substantial possessions, or property. If you dream that others around you are naked, you may find that in waking life you will soon discover that a person is not being his or her true self with you.

NEEDLES

Needles, like most other pointed objects in dreams, are often a
warning of some danger or obstacle. Whether it is a sewing needle
or a pine needle, a sharp needle generally represents pain or the fear
of pain.

Dreaming of threading a needle is symbolic of a particular
venture that requires either mending, construction, or some other
form of industriousness. If you dream that you thread a needle
easily, you will be successful in your venture and will not have too
many obstacles to contend with.

If you have trouble seeing the eye of the needle and find it
difficult to thread the needle without aid, you may require some
help to finish your project or you may need to have light shed on
some particular details which are preventing
the project's completion. Carelessness with a
needle is considered a bad omen—a dream
of pricking your finger represents the bad
luck of another affecting your plans. Losing
a needle indicates danger coming your way
because of your carelessness.

NIGHTMARES

FOR A DISCUSSION OF **NIGHTMARES**, SEE PAGE 168.
SEE ALSO **FEARS**, PAGE 66.

NOSES

To dream of a very large and broad nose suggests that you are
directing yourself toward gain and attainment. A swollen nose is
indicates success in business; a small nose indicates a change for the
better in terms of your prosperity.

A runny nose suggests that certain knowledge, if kept secret, will
promote success. A blocked nose signifies obstacles coming your
way from either family or close friends. Blowing your nose may
mean that your responsibilities and obligations will lessen.

Watch out for dreams about having a cold nose—this is
traditionally a warning against being unfaithful.

O

OCEANS

A dream in which you find yourself on a shore looking out over the sea indicates your preoccupation with emotional issues—the mood of the ocean reflects your own mood. For example, a calm bright sea indicates self-confidence and a preparedness to take on new adventures; a sullen gray ocean, depression; a storm-tossed sea, extreme emotional turmoil; a darkened ocean, a lack of understanding of your needs and feelings; and a brightly moonlit seascape, a sense of romance and mystery. Tidal waves in dreams generally represent the release of emotion and tension.

If you view the ocean from a cliff-top or a building in your dream, you may be feeling emotionally distant. Watching waves crashing against rocks usually indicates that you are emotionally under siege. Walking along a calm beach, on the other hand, signifies emotional contentment and expansiveness.

Swimming, especially skinny-dipping, suggests spiritual cleansing, and emerging from the sea after bathing suggests rebirth (see also *Nakedness*, page 112). Diving into the sea represents a need for decisive action. Snorkeling, scuba diving, or magically being able to swim without surfacing suggests an interest in spirituality, psychology, or the supernatural (see also *Underwater*, page 150).

Hearing the sound of waves and seabirds from a distance and smelling salty air without actually seeing the ocean suggests that something is enticing you to travel and have an adventure.

Dreams of ocean travel should be interpreted according to the sailing conditions. Journeying across a calm ocean is an extremely good omen for all aspects of the future, though an extremely long trip may suggest a period of life lacking in change for either better or worse. Sailing a stormy sea is, of course, symbolic of dangers. If the embattled journey is a business trip, look to your finances and career; if it is a pleasure cruise, relationship troubles are looming.

OFFICES

Finding yourself in an office in a dream often indicates a tendency to be overly preoccupied with business and financial matters, particularly if your career in the waking world keeps you in that sort of environment.
Dreaming of your own office generally indicates excessive job pressure—consider taking a holiday as soon as you can. An exception to this is a dream in which you are taking pleasure in the job for its own sake and excelling in your line of business. This might still indicate the need for a more rounded life, but it does show that you feel confident in professional matters.

If you do not work in an office, a dream in this sort of setting often suggests bureaucratic or financial entanglements that are taking time and energy away from your usual job or interests.

OUT-OF-BODY DREAMS

Dreams in which you feel not connected with your body, or in which you seem to be on an astral plane, can indicate that your spirit is seeking renewal or wishes to access its past or future, or to observe the present from the astral perspective.

Your nonphysical self will often be able to fly, pass through objects, and remain undetected by anyone else—all these indicate your need for much more freedom.

Occasionally, having such a dream expresses your desire to see how others react when they are unaware of your presence. This indicates a lack of trust in others and an undermined sense of self-confidence.

If an out-of-body dream seems particularly vivid, jot down the details of everything you have seen and heard as soon as you wake and check its accuracy later in the day. The dream just might have been reality!

■ FOR **PAINS**, SEE **ACCIDENTS**, PAGE 25.

PAINTING

A dream in which you or someone else draw, paint, or sculpt might be regarded as a subconscious expression of the need to be creative. Traditionally, painting a picture suggests that changes are occurring in your life—new opportunities will soon become available.

If you are painting with a heavy medium, such as oils, using the paint thickly and lushly, you will experience major, profitable changes; if you are painting with diluted paint, such as watercolors, you will make only small shifts in your work—you may still be inhibited by feelings of inadequacy or some other fear.

If you are painting furniture using cans of paint you may be experimenting with an idea that you are not yet ready to share. However, if you are applying gilt, gold leaf, or some other decorative finish, you may be attracting a new lover or admirer.

Dreams of painting a house indicate that you wish to keep some information secret until you have thought out all the ramifications.

PALACES

Dreaming of seeing the exterior of a palace indicates that your fortunes will rise. However, dreaming of the luxurious interior of a palace suggests that your thoughts outstrip the reality of the

situation—you may have an overinflated opinion of yourself or another person, or believe that a particular opportunity is much better than it really is. As a consequence of not seeing things as they truly are, you may generate hostility and suffer a lack of support.

◼ FOR **PALMS**, SEE **BODIES**, PAGE 36, AND **HANDS**, PAGE 79.

◼ FOR **PALM TREES**, SEE **GARDENS**, PAGE 74.

PARALYSIS

Dreams of paralysis are believed by some to be an indication of alien abduction, even though such dreams occurred for centuries before being linked with aliens. Traditionally, a paralysis dream is symbolic of a fear that is repressing your ability to move or do anything constructive. This fear basically stems from emotional turmoil, including sexual inhibitions.

Such dreams may be symptomatic of your feeling overwhelmed with responsibilities or deadlines in your waking life, and therefore feeling seized up and unable to proceed. If you have recurring dreams of paralysis, discuss this dream sequence with a counselor and make an appointment with your doctor to have a general checkup. Paralysis dreams could also be the result of problems with your circulation.

◼ FOR **PARENTS**, SEE **FATHERS**, PAGE 65,

AND **MOTHERS**, PAGE 109.

PARKS

SEE ALSO **GARDENS**, PAGE 74, AND **PLAYGROUNDS**, PAGE 120.

Dreaming that you are walking through or playing in a park usually reflects balance in the family, at home, with yourself, and with the people around you. It is a dream of contentment if the park seems well tended and sunny. If the park contains a playground that appears poorly maintained and flower beds that are unkempt, you may be about to go through a troubled, lonely time.

If the park has a maze that you enter, your subconscious may be searching for answers and trying to understand changes that are occurring in your life. You might find the end of the maze in your dream once your conscious mind has found the answers to your questions. Mazes show you that you need to stop running around in circles—you need to stay still and determine what you want out of life.

PARTIES

SEE ALSO **INVITATIONS**, PAGE 89.

When you dream of a party, make a note in your dream journal as to whether you enjoyed yourself or not. If you are happy at the party and feel comfortable with the situation and with the people you are meeting, you will find that you are resolving issues in your waking life around your friends and that you are coming to a stage in your life when you are truly enjoying your social circle.

If you dream that you are not happy at the party, you may need to do some more work on improving communication with your

friends and family. Note exactly what it is that makes you feel uncomfortable at the party—is it a particular person, or do you feel embarrassed about the attention you are given or not given?

If you can determine what has made you unhappy at the event, note it in your dream journal and

find a way of dealing with the issue. For example, if you feel that you are constantly being judged, work on feeling that you do not need to measure up to anybody's standards but your own.

Traditionally, if you dream that you are at a party because you have been invited, you will experience an increase in opportunities to make new friends and to network effectively. If you dream of giving a lavish party, however, you may be the focus of some gossip and unfair comment.

PEARLS

Pearls are believed to be dream images of teardrops; they usually indicate that you are going through a grieving process or fear being overemotional. Traditionally, dreams of a pearl necklace are believed to presage a stroke of incredibly good luck.

PERFORMANCES

Seeing yourself onstage performing in a
dream might mean that you are not being
yourself in your real life. Perhaps you are
projecting an image of what you believe
others expect and you are being judged on
that false image. If there is no one in the

audience, you might be letting yourself know that you are unhappy
with the situation.

Performing before an audience may also indicate that you are
expecting to be judged on your performance. A dream in which you
feel comfortable on the stage, and in command of the audience, is
usually an indication that you are ready for whatever appraisal or
audition is coming up in your real life. If you feel uncomfortable
and exposed on your dream stage, you may need to do a bit more
preparation.

A stage may also be symbolic of your attempts to improve your
situation, as you are appearing elevated in front of your audience.

Dreaming of acting may signify that you are unable to express
your emotions directly to someone. Make a note in your dream
journal of any member of the audience you recognize. If you see
someone you know, the dream may be an indication that you need
to work on communicating with that particular person or type of
person in order to resolve feelings of frustration or anger.

A common anxiety dream is being onstage and forgetting your
words or what you have to do. This kind of dream suggests that you
may feel that people—or circumstances—are repressing you so
much that you forget what you really should be doing.

■ FOR **PERFUMES**, SEE **SMELLS**, PAGE 135.

PLAYGROUNDS

SEE ALSO **PARKS**, PAGE 117.

Dreaming of a playground is often a sign that you are considering your future. If the playground is well kept and all the equipment works, is well oiled, and does not make a sound in the wind or when you are using it, a successful future is assured—you have already taken the necessary steps to ensure this.

However, if the equipment is in bad repair, you may need to make an active effort to prepare for what you would like your future to be.

A dream of an empty, slowly swaying swing might suggest contemplating different points of view. Playing on the swing represents being able to understand these varied perspectives.

Watching children play or laughing is believed to be an omen of good luck. If you are playing as a child, this represents your desire or need to find your inner child and to balance the load of responsibilities that you may be feeling.

A merry-go-round is symbolic of the circle of life, so dreaming of happily playing on the merry-go-round means you are feeling equally happy about the cycles and phases of your life. However, if the merry-go-round is in poor repair or you are the only one riding on it, you may be experiencing some disappointments in your life.

■ FOR **POLICEMEN**, SEE **CRIMES**, PAGE 48.

PRECIOUS AND SEMIPRECIOUS GEMS

Dreaming of wearing or acquiring a precious or semiprecious gem suggests that you are being given—or are becoming attuned to— a particular type of spiritual guidance that will help you achieve your goals.

Each stone has its own traditional associations, but your own feelings as you are wearing the gem are the most important guide as to what that gem means for you. Make a note in your dream journal if you can capture this feeling in your dream. Here are a number of general dream associations for gems.

- Amethysts—you will soon receive some unexpected news that will give you a sense of contentment and peace.
- Diamonds—you will soon receive a modest amount of money from an unexpected source.
- Emeralds—you will find a way of overcoming obstacles and delays.
- Jade—you will feel protected and prosperous when wearing this stone.
- Rubies—you will attract passion and love.

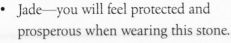
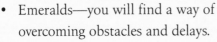
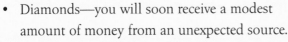

PREGNANCY

SEE ALSO **BIRTHS**, PAGE 35.

A dream of pregnancy can suggest two different things: that you believe in growth or that your inner fears are being resolved. Traditionally, dreams of being pregnant are believed to presage an increase in material possessions or wealth.

However, if you feel unhappy about the pregnancy in the dream, perhaps you feel that you cannot handle the responsibility of this increase in wealth. Wealth brings with it added burdens and problems that may get in the way of your path, particularly if you are focused on a spiritual direction. If you feel happy about the pregnancy, then you are ready to accept these added burdens, and will find new joy and fulfillment.

R

RAILROADS

Seeing a railroad line in a dream suggests that you are following a steady path toward your chosen destination. If you see yourself walking along the line, you are showing a desire to do things on your own terms, at your own rate, and with no interference from others.

Dreaming that you are catching a train generally indicates that you are on schedule for something that you want to be doing; missing a train by a few minutes indicates fear that you have left important issues unattended until too late. Dreaming that you are waiting in a station usually signifies your confidence that the

opportunities you need to continue with or complete a project will soon present themselves. Riding a train without a ticket suggests that you feel mildly guilty about a certain course of action.

Dreams involving train travel suggest steady progress, with no likely obstructions to success. A blockage on the track or a derailment, however, can warn of delays or upsets to plans you felt were entirely under control. A train passing over a bridge predicts an effortless triumph over obstacles, while passing through a tunnel suggests continued advancement through unknown territory (see also *Tunnels*, page 148).

Different types of trains also have particular meanings. A steam train suggests that a gentle, old-fashioned approach to a pressing issue will prove effective, while a fast electric train suggests that decisiveness and speed are the principal requirements.

Underground rail journeys are a sign that you should keep your progress to yourself rather than parading it before the world. Dreaming of a crowded commuter train often symbolizes your frustration at being treated impersonally; dreaming of a freight train suggests that a task will only be completed through a long, steady haul.

RAIN

Dreams involving rain often refer to the need for emotional release. If the rain is soft and gentle, this release will be a peaceful and gradual expression of unwanted emotions that will leave the mind feeling cleansed and open to new possibilities.

Heavy rain suggests that you are feeling overloaded with unreleased feelings, particularly grief. Thunderstorms indicate that a powerful release of emotion is imminent, and that unpleasant as it may feel at the time, it will leave you feeling much happier. Thunder without rain, on the other hand, symbolizes a steady increase in tensions with no release in sight.

Being safely inside, out of the rain or storm, in a dream usually suggests that you have found some form of sanctuary from life's upsets. If the shelter is only temporary or leaks, you may have little faith in this sanctuary's permanence. If, on the other hand, you are sitting by a warm fire cozily sipping tea while a storm rages outside, the sanctuary is a secure part of your emotional makeup.

To dream of being caught in an unexpected shower suggests that lack of foresight is a common problem for you; struggling through a heavy rainstorm indicates that you have a brave and determined nature. If you dream of strolling through a warm summer shower, the dream may symbolize your emotional resilience and ability to handle problems in a cheerful and optimistic way. Being caught in a cold, drenching downpour is a warning against looming health problems, but standing or walking naked in gentle rain indicates a cleansing of the heart and the spirit.

Seeing a rainbow at the end of a shower symbolizes unexpectedly renewed hope and good fortune—even if you don't find a pot of gold at the rainbow's end.

■ FOR **RAVENS**, SEE **BIRDS**, PAGE 34.

■ FOR **RELATIVES**, SEE **FATHERS**, PAGE 65, **MOTHERS**, PAGE 109, AND **SIBLINGS**, PAGE 134.

RELIGION

SEE ALSO **HEAVEN OR HELL** IN **ALIENS AND OTHERWORLDLY ENTITIES**, PAGE 27.

The interpretation of religious imagery in dreams will vary according to each person's spiritual beliefs. Certain religious symbolism, however, seems to crop up in most of our dreams from time to time.

Tempting (or worrying) as it may be, dreaming of meeting extremely powerful spiritual beings, such as saints, angels, the Buddha, Christ, the Virgin Mary, and so on, should not necessarily be interpreted as a genuinely divine encounter. In the majority of cases, the religious figure in question will be, like most dreamed entities, the creation of your dreaming self. Such dreams should, however, be given special attention, because your subconscious is trying to give you a very important message.

Often your depiction of such personages represents your need to be accepted and loved by your perception of a higher being, and your interaction with such beings in your dreams will instruct you on how to change your life to become worthy of such acceptance.

DREAM FACT

*One of the first dream psychologists
Fritz Perl (1893–1970)*

An Austrian psychiatrist and one of the founders of Gestalt therapy, Fritz Perl viewed all characters and situations in our lives as disowned aspects of ourselves. He encouraged his clients to role-play and give voice in words and body language to the people and symbols in their dreams. By acting out what these elements were communicating, the dreamer could tap into the meaning of the dream and the different parts of his or her personality, and integrate them into a whole. The Gestalt approach adds a level of consciousness to the dream state. Many people still find this method effective today.

REPTILES

Snakes, lizards, and other small, venomous animals often—rather unfairly to the actual creatures—represent uncertainty and deceit. They usually appear in your dreams at times when you suspect someone is not to be trusted or when you feel you are being secretly persecuted, unfairly judged, or excluded.

Reptiles might visit your dreams when you are not voicing your opinions. Often they also represent conflict with an overbearing person or someone whose behavior is unacceptable or whose standards you are unwilling to meet.

However, a dream image of a crocodile or alligator, traditional symbols of the jaws of justice, is usually a reminder of some wrongdoing that you cannot admit to yourself or others.

RINGS

SEE ALSO **JEWELRY**, PAGES 90–91.

Because of their central role in marriage rituals, rings traditionally symbolize commitment and union, whether romantic, creative, or professional. Their circular shape, with neither beginning nor end, suggests constancy and mutual trust.

A plain golden ring represents simple, unadorned fidelity, while a more flamboyant bejeweled ring represents a more public statement of affection. An overly flashy ring, however, may signify an insincere relationship. A signet ring often suggests that you are putting your own interests ahead of those of anyone else.

Dreaming of being given or finding a ring suggests a bright future for whatever partnership is most important to you at the time. Losing or breaking a ring is obviously much less auspicious; it suggests that a major relationship, business or emotional, is on rocky ground. To dream of removing or discarding a ring is a clear indication that you are ready to move into a new phase of your life.

If you find that a ring has become stuck on your finger in your dream, a past relationship may still be a dominating emotional force; alternatively, it may indicate problems involving some form of (possibly unrecognized) addiction. A ring that is either too tight or too loose indicates that there are areas of incompatibility in a current or impending relationship that need to be addressed.

RIVERS

Rivers frequently symbolize the dreamer's spiritual life. A river typically begins as a spring bubbling from the earth, makes a rapid turbulent trip down from the heights, mingles its waters with other streams, slows down, widens and becomes more substantial as it nears sea level, then empties into the ocean.

The water molecules may then spend vast spans of time as part of the ocean or be evaporated by the sun's heat and taken back into the clouds, which rain onto the earth, nourishing the spring water that feeds new rivers.

This cycle has struck spiritual thinkers for generations as a perfect metaphor for the existence of individual souls, with the river phase representing our earthly life and the ocean phase our continued existence in higher realms of being.

Dreaming of watching a river flowing past suggests that you have a degree of calm, content detachment from everyday life; traveling gently along a stream by boat or raft represents an equally serene approach to life. To have your romantic partner aboard the vessel shows confidence and pleasure in the fact that your two life-paths have merged.

Encountering obstacles such as rapids or, more alarmingly, waterfalls while boating down the river can reflect difficulties you are currently facing or signal that there are difficulties ahead. The scale of the obstacle will indicate your feelings about the problem.

Springs and young streams often represent childhood; broad, busy rivers, such as the Mississippi, the prime of one's working life; and river mouths, the contentment of old age.

■ FOR **ROBBERIES**, SEE **CRIMES**, PAGE 48.

ROYALTY

SEE ALSO **FAMOUS PEOPLE**, PAGE 64.

By some accounts, the most frequently encountered celebrity in humanity's dreams throughout the last century has been Queen Elizabeth II, which indicates that regardless of the changing role of royalty in our culture, the institution remains extremely powerful in our subconscious lives.

A dream of a harmonious encounter with royalty, whether an actual monarch, living or dead, or an imagined figure, indicates a desire to be accepted by someone who both stands above the mass of humanity and represents its aspirations. Symbolically, to be praised by royalty is to be praised by the entire world.

Often, however, these royal encounters in dreams are marred by some inappropriate comment on the dreamer's part or a breach of regal etiquette. In these dreams, imperial disapproval becomes an equally potent symbol of the dreamer's fear of universal disfavor or ridicule.

To dream of yourself as royalty may symbolize your confidence and self-assurance, but it may just as easily reveal a snobbish, social-climbing side of yourself that you would rather not acknowledge. We should all be wary of needing to feel superior to everyone else before we can approve of our own lives.

Dreaming of others being elevated to royal status often indicates that you feel inferior to them and may envy certain qualities they exhibit that you are unable to find in yourself. The message of such a dream is usually that you must try harder to nurture your own potential, rather than settling for a life lived in the shadows of your supposed betters.

■ FOR **RUNNING**, SEE **CHASING**, PAGE 41.

SCHOOLS

If you dream that you are back in school, in your wakened state you might be feeling that you have much to learn. This would be a natural dream if you have embarked on a new career or are moving in a new life direction. It could also mean that you need to choose or move into a direction more suited to your personality and goals.

You may also be finding that you are being held back by not letting go of the past, and that there are elements in your past that need resolution. Were you bullied at school or were you the school bully? You may need to focus on your feelings of vulnerability or anger before you can feel a sense of fulfillment.

If you dream about a teacher, you may be suffering an inner imbalance or a health problem. It may also be an indication that

you feel you are being led into a situation you are not happy about. However, if you dream of a favorite teacher whom you trust, listen closely to what the teacher has to say to you.

An image of yourself as a teacher generally indicates that you have grown and want to share your knowledge with others. This may be a good omen for people seeking to write or lecture about their area(s) of expertise.

Being in a school playground or near a school is an indication that you may soon receive some unexpected money.

If you dream that you are walking in the corridors of the school without any direction, or that you seem to be lost in a school, you may need to focus on finding your true path in life.

SCISSORS

A pair of scissors in a dream suggests that something is catching up with you or you are finding it difficult to keep pace with a trying situation. If you dream that you are buying or using scissors, you realize that you need to show some precision in your thinking or about your work at the moment. If you feel that you are not currently being meticulous or precise about certain important details, this is a warning that you need to do that if you are to achieve your goals.

If you dream that you and your lover are using the same pair of scissors, you may be heading toward an argument about your relationship. As in superstition, it is considered bad luck to dream about receiving scissors as a gift. Note in your dream journal if you can remember who sent you a pair of scissors—you may find that you need to resolve some issues with that person.

SCOLDING

This unpleasant dream is a warning that you may be feeling unjustly confident about a particular situation. To help you work out which area of your life you feel overconfident about, try to remember and note in your dream journal who is doing the scolding. If it is a parent, you may be about to make an unwise decision or an unfair assumption concerning your family. If you are the one doing the scolding, consider being more diplomatic in your waking life.

SCRATCHING OR BEING SCRATCHED

SEE **BODIES**, PAGE 36, FOR DREAM ASSOCIATIONS CONCERNING VARIOUS PARTS OF THE BODY.

Dreaming that you are scratching a particular part of your body indicates that you may feel pain in that area or that you feel emotionally hurt by a particular situation.

Traditionally, it is believed that if you scratch your back in a dream, you may receive some unexpected money.

SCREAMING

Traditionally, screaming in your dream is believed to have a contrary meaning—it is an omen of good fortune for you and those around you in the dream who hear your screams.

Take note of why you are screaming, as this could be an indication that you need to release tension about a certain situation or circumstance, or that you should vent your feelings in your waking life rather than bottling them up. Repressed emotions are known to have repercussions on a person's health, so consider letting go of your emotions in a safe place.

SCULPTURES

Seeing sculptures of people in your dreams is associated with atrophy and emotional shutdown; your dream is warning you that you might need to break through your frozen emotions and reconnect with the people around you. If you dream of a famous sculpture, you may need to incorporate something that the sculpture reminds you of into your life—this might help you unlock your repressed emotions. However, if you dream that you are  the one creating the sculpture, you may be in control of the process of sculpting your life into a new shape. Traditionally, dreaming of being a sculptor indicates a vibrant, creative change in direction.

SEEDS

Seeds are dream symbols of new beginnings and opportunities. If you dream that you are sowing seeds, make a note of where you are sowing them. If the ground seems fertile, your seeds will grow well and your new directions will flourish. Dreaming that you have scattered the seeds on barren soil or on concrete may indicate, if you feel purposeful or pleased in the dream, that you are able to make something out of a previously unproductive idea or relationship. If you are feeling regret as you scatter the seeds, you may be wasting your time on something or someone.

■ FOR **SEMIPRECIOUS GEMS OR STONES**, SEE **PRECIOUS AND SEMIPRECIOUS GEMS**, PAGE 121.

SEX

Sexual dreams sometimes occur if you are unhappy because of a lack of sexual activity or because of the quality of sexual activity in your life. Such dreams might enable you to release the tensions and experience some of the pleasure that is not available to you in your conscious life.

Having an orgasm during a dream is thought to be a way of restoring balance in your life. Remember, we are all physical, emotional, mental, and spiritual beings, and sexuality is a part of the self that needs to be acknowledged. Dreams are often the only way we do this.

If you dream that you are enjoying the sexual experience, this is traditionally believed to indicate that you are feeling happy with your life at the moment.

If a woman dreams of a penis, she might be feeling sexually frustrated or sexually attracted to a man. If she dreams she has a penis, she might be unable to express herself as she would wish, or be frustrated by her own limitations. If a man dreams of a penis, it might relate to feelings of either superiority or inferiority. If a man dreams of being afraid that someone will see his penis, it is possible that he is afraid of being vulnerable.

Sometimes dreams about sex have little to do with the sexual act. They may indicate the need for you to rebalance the male and female aspects of your personality. Often, dreaming about having sex with someone may mean you are in a nurturing situation with that person. You may be merging in some way with that person, or opening yourself up to him or her.

SHADOWS

Seeing your own shadow in a dream indicates a sense of acute vulnerability, a dislike of your body, or a fear that you won't be accepted by others. It may also be an indication that you must face the dark side of your personality and resolve any issues that are upsetting you. The shadow is believed to be the primal part of our psyche, the part that deals with intense emotions.

If your shadow is not connected to you in the dream, you may be feeling that you have not integrated or resolved some strong emotion. If your shadow is connected to you in the normal way, the dream indicates success in legal matters or the acquisition of an inheritance—the shadow is symbolic of the world of the dead touching you beneficially.

Seeing another person's shadow may mean that you are out of touch with what you want in life and are unable to see what is being presented to you by others. Traditionally, such a dream is considered a warning against traveling in the immediate future.

■ FOR **SHARKS**, SEE **FISH AND OTHER SEA CREATURES** ON PAGES 68–69.

DREAM FACT

The teachings of Carl Jung

Carl Jung argued that our conscious and subconscious minds should not be seen as opposites, but as complementary parts of our natural, healthy psyche. He advised that to maintain psychological equilibrium, we would do well to allow the two to work together. Jung held dreams to be direct manifestations of our deepest, most natural instincts for well-being, and to be reliable guides to reality, projecting a true picture—a picture that our conscious minds might attempt to deny or fail to recognize. Jung also maintained that dreams could supply solutions as well as delivering insights.

SHIPS

SEE ALSO **OCEANS**, PAGE 114.

Ships are traditionally symbols of success in business. The more ships you see, either in port or as a fleet, the more successful your business venture. To determine the type of business in which you will find such success, make a note in your  dream journal of what your ships are carrying, if you can remember. If they carry people, you may be successful in a service business; if they carry a cargo of certain goods, such a product or type of product may lead you to success.

Sea travel may also represent excitement about the future. Make a note about the state of the sea—is it calm, choppy, or rough? Is the ship having trouble getting to its destination? If it is, there may be some delays before you achieve success.

Dreaming that you are standing on a dock, watching a boat depart, may indicate that you are missing out on an activity you want to be involved in. A boating accident might represent a cancellation of some scheduled event.

SHOPPING MALLS

Dream images of shopping malls generally signify the process of transition from a smaller to a larger social or professional group. This type of image might occur when you have many new things confronting you at once and are unable to deal with them all. A very dark shopping mall might represent a big change in your life that you are uncertain about. A dream that you are alone or with strangers in a shopping mall suggests a move to a new environment. If you are working in the shopping mall—or in any sort of shop— you may be lucky with money at the moment. Feel free to use this in your waking life!

SIBLINGS

Dreams about you and your siblings getting along well generally indicate a new period of harmony and understanding developing within your family.

Dreaming of your sister, if you are a female, is traditionally believed to mean that you still need to resolve a certain disagreement. To identify the argument your dream refers to, note in your dream journal what clues are given—for example, try to remember what your sister was wearing or holding. If you dream of your brother, you may be entering a phase of domestic stability.

If you are a male, dreaming of your sister usually indicates family contentment; dreaming of a harmonious relationship with your brother is symbolic of financial or business success. However, if you and your brother are fighting in your dream, you may find that domestic arguments seem to flare up over nothing in your waking life.

Seeing a sibling walk through fire or against a background of fire might reflect your awareness of your brother or sister's personal growth and strength of mind, your pride in them, and the security you feel in the relationship.

SLEEP

If you have dreamed that you are sleeping on a particular surface or with a particular person, make a note in your dream journal of the dream situation, and try to remember who was beside you on the bed and what the bed was made of.

Dreaming of sleeping next to your wife or husband symbolizes marital harmony; dreaming of sleeping with your lover can indicate that you feel uncertain about him or her. A dream in which there are animals on the bed may be an omen of accidents. Dreams of sleeping with a stranger may indicate that you feel embarrassment about confiding information to someone you don't really know.

Dreaming that you are sleeping on a mattress or a couple of blankets that appear to be made of wool indicates achievement of your goals, while sleeping on sand represents a shifting of opportunities which may lead to discouragement or disappointment.

SMELLS

Smells are generally straightforward in their dream associations. Being aware of an unpleasant odor in a dream usually suggests dental problems, but occasionally it signifies illness. It could also indicate that something does not "smell right" about a certain person or project. Note in your dream journal what you were looking at when you first smelled the bad odor.

Follow your instincts in waking life about what your dream is indicating. It may be that a certain person is not emotionally well or stable but you are not aware of it yet. Alternatively, perhaps there is not enough money circulating in your business venture and it is going to stall through lack of funds.

Pleasant odors usually represent a reward for accomplishment and are believed to be omens of good luck and fortune. Identifying certain smells and perfumes may give you further information about what they signify. For example, if the scent is one that your mother wears, you may feel nurture and love infusing your dream, indicating perhaps that you are supported in your dream and your waking life. If the odor is the aftershave your father uses, your venture may be given his blessing and you may find that you have significant material success.

Smelling the perfumes of certain flowers connects with the usual dream associations for these flowers. For instance:

- hyacinths—domestic contentment
- jasmine—success in love
- lavender—harmony and balance
- lilies—social success
- roses—joy and happiness.

SNOW

Snow is traditionally an omen of good
luck and fortune. The pure white of
freshly fallen snow is symbolic of
success. Even if you dream of trudging
through the snow, you may find that
you will, through hard work, receive a
substantial reward.

There is usually a sense of joy and wonder when snow first falls,
so dreaming that the snow has come early in the year (for instance,
in fall) may suggest that you will experience happiness from an
unexpected source. If snow falls in spring, you may have unexpected
success in your business or your finances. Snow falling in summer
predicts a secure and profitable business year, while snow falling
when it should—in winter—may indicate minor, temporary
financial setbacks.

The only bad omen concerning snow is if you dream that you
are eating it. Ingesting the coldness of the snow symbolizes a lack of
warmth in your life and warns you of a period of sadness ahead.

SOUNDS

SEE ALSO **LAUGHTER**, PAGE 97, AND **MUSIC**, PAGE 111.

Sounds are an important part of your dream vocabulary, and
outside sounds can easily intrude on your dreams, sometimes
snapping you awake or being incorporated into your dream before
you finally wake up. For example, if you are asleep and the
telephone rings, your dream may start accommodating the sounds
by providing images of you talking on the
telephone.

Sharp, distracting sounds in a dream
typically represent conflict and confusion
in your conscious life. Melodious,
harmonious sounds may indicate a sense
of balance and contentment in your life.

SPECIAL POWERS OR ABILITIES

SEE ALSO **INVISIBILITY**, PAGE 89, OR **FLYING**, PAGE 72.

Dreaming that you possess enhanced or superhuman abilities may symbolize a subconscious release of frustration at a lack of ability or physical strength to accomplish some task or feat in your waking life.

However, if you are using your new skills, powers, or abilities as if they are second nature to you in your dream, you may soon have opportunities to achieve your goals and develop enough confidence to gain success and recognition.

Make a note in your dream journal of any clues given in the dream about how to shift your perception so that you can achieve what you want.

Having superhuman abilities can also simply indicate how you need to feel in order to overcome any feelings of restriction in your waking life.

SPHINXES

Dreaming of a sphinx, a creature with the body of a lion and the head of a man (the ancient Egyptian symbol of the pharaoh, representing wisdom and mystery), is believed to be a contrary dream—it indicates that you will soon find a solution to your problems. This dream is designed to give you the confidence to focus on your particular problem and to understand that the solution is not necessarily one that comes to mind easily. There is a puzzle or riddle for you to unravel if you have patience and devote some time to its solution.

SPIDERS

Large, dark spiders in a dream usually signify a change for the better, a reward after a period of famine or financial troubles—it's a contrary dream. How good the omen is depends on the size of the spider: the bigger, the better! However, there is one exception to this rule—seeing a tarantula indicates the onset of health worries.

A purple or lavender hue around a spider indicates a spiritual gift, possibly from your spirit guide. A red-backed spider suggests that there will be a price to pay for something you desire. A yellow-striped spider indicates that you will receive a reward for your work. Other colors generally signify that you do not accurately understand the value or purpose of an offer that has been made to you (see also *Colors*, pages 44–47).

Dead spiders suggest fear or uncertainty. As soon as possible after you dream of squashing a spider, consciously affirm that you wish to release any fear of the spider and accept its particular gift to you. Images of concealed spiders might signify your fear of the future.

When spiders are swinging from a web in your dreams, it is likely that good fortune will enter your life. Spiders resting in a web suggest a need for comfortable accommodation. If a spider is

entangled in a web, you may be uncomfortable in your sleeping place or stifled in your daily life.

Cobwebs alone are usually symbols of wealth, prosperity, and a change for the better in your circumstances.

DREAM TIP

Being chased

If you dream that you are being chased, try to remember in your dream that you are only dreaming—turn around to face and confront whatever is chasing you. This will usually put an end to dreams of this kind.

STARS

SEE ALSO **COLORS**, PAGES 44–47, IF THE
LIGHT FROM THE STAR IS NOT THE USUAL WHITE HUE.

Stars shining brightly are usually symbols of the early flickering of new ideas. Dim and minuscule stars might indicate some difficulty with eyesight or headaches.

Traditionally, stars in dreams can represent either good luck or misfortune. Seeing a shooting star is lucky, and dreaming of looking  up at the stars may mean you will get some important news soon—perhaps the stars symbolize your need to obtain an answer or solution to a particular problem and your feeling that the answer must come from a place beyond your immediate world.

Seeing a star shining brightly in the sky presages obstacles and delays in business, and starlight shining into your room may indicate a spiritual transformation.

■ FOR **STOMACHS**, SEE **BODIES**, PAGE 36.

STRENGTH

Feeling strong in a dream is an indication that you have the power within you to accomplish great feats, either physically or mentally. If you are feeling physically weakened at the moment, note in your dream journal how it felt to feel so strong. This type of dream is a reminder that you have power within you—you just need to remember to use it.

Traditionally, dreams of strength have had contrary meanings— they suggest that your ambitions outstrip your capabilities. However, you can always improve your skills; it is just a matter of focus and confidence.

If you are struggling with someone or something, your dream may be suggesting that you will conquer certain issues that have been bothering you. If you are struggling with a ferocious animal, you are going to experience a lucky phase of your life.

SURF AND SURFING

SEE ALSO **OCEANS**, PAGE 114.

Feeling that you are riding a wave indicates that you are using the circumstances of your life well and that you have adapted well to the changing situation. If you feel comfortable and in control, this dream is a good omen—you have entered a phase of your life where you are at the height of your powers.

If you feel otherwise in waking life, take note in your dream journal of how it felt to have such control and adaptability. Try to incorporate some flexibility in the way you do things in waking life and trust in your abilities.

If you are watching the surf roll onto the sand in your dream, some benefits will also roll in virtually at your feet. A sum of money or some opportunities may soon appear.

SWAMPS

The primal stench and stagnation of a swamp is a warning against stagnation in your own life—which may be the result of not having enough money, or of being with people who are not forward thinking or are in some way holding you back. This dream may be telling you that you need to assess whether or not you should end certain relationships and refrain from buying more than you can afford to at the moment. When you remove the stagnation from your life, you will find that money and beneficial friendships will again flow to you easily.

SWEARING

Uttering profanities is generally considered an unfortunate omen. If a man is swearing at you in your dream, you may find that your income suffers slightly; if a woman speaks such words, you may be involved in a dead-end love affair that could cause you humiliation and embarrassment.

SWEEPING

The action of sweeping usually symbolizes something being cleared from your life. If you dream that you are sweeping a floor, take note of what kind of floor is it and where it is. For instance, if you are sweeping in the family room or a kitchen, where the family usually gathers, you may be clearing away past grievances and unhappiness from the home to allow new understanding to flow in. If you are sweeping in your study or workplace, you may see an increase in your finances.

SWIMMING

SEE ALSO **OCEANS**, PAGE 114, AND **WATER**, PAGE 158.

Swimming in a pool is considered unlucky, and an indication that your actions are being undermined by a particular person. However, swimming in the sea suggests that you will have success in business after an initial struggle.

Swimming in the nude is traditionally considered an omen of good luck. It is symbolic of you becoming part of the world around you, feeling comfortable and free to do what you want.

If you dream of teaching someone to swim, you may have a stroke of good luck in your finances; your generosity in sharing your knowledge in your dream may indicate that you will be rewarded in your waking life.

SWORDS

SEE ALSO **KNIVES**, PAGE 95.

Like the dream associations of other sharp objects, dreaming of a keen-bladed, serviceable sword is generally a warning of bad news and discouragement ahead. Seeing a sword is a sign of bad news; seeing a broken sword signals major disappointment. However, being hurt by a sword is traditionally a contrary dream—good luck and success in business will soon come your way.

T

■ FOR **TABLES**, SEE **FURNITURE**, PAGE 73.

TEETH

The experience of losing teeth in our childhood seems to make quite an impression on our subconscious minds—the imagery frequently crops up in our dreams. If your physical teeth are reasonably strong and healthy, the loss of teeth in your dreams symbolizes a stage of growth and deepening maturity. It may also predict that imagined worries are passing.

Similarly, when you dream that you are developing teeth, you are usually on the brink of greater self-knowledge and wisdom or approaching a spiritual path to inner peace.

Dreaming that you have developed sharper or longer teeth sometimes indicates your uneasiness with certain primal aspects of your nature. Seeing bestial or extremely damaged or rotten teeth in the mouth of someone else during a dream is a warning to be suspicious of someone's malicious or deceitful words.

Dreams involving dental discomfort may be a way to tell you that you are grinding your teeth while dreaming, because of stress, suppressed anger, or anxiety, or poor neck or jaw alignment.

TELEPHONES

A telephone in your dream suggests that you are waiting for information or are anxious for communication from a distant loved one. It is also not uncommon to dream of talking to a recently deceased relative or friend on the phone, perhaps because you feel they are still willing to communicate with you despite their invisibility to your waking eyes.

A dream in which you are making business calls suggests overwork and an inability to disconnect from your career even in sleep. Constant use of cell phones in dreams indicates that you have insecurities about your friendships and a need for constant reassurance of your importance to others. Persistent phone ringing in a dream symbolizes frequent interruptions to your concentration.

You may hear a phone ringing in your dream because your phone is actually ringing and your dream has incorporated the sound (see also *Sounds*, page 136).

Phone malfunctions in your dreams are a clear symbol of communication problems with important people in your waking life.

TEMPLES

A dream about a temple usually indicates that you need some kind of enhancement of your spiritual life. If the temple in your dream is the sort of neglected, dusty, cobweb-covered arrangement you might imagine Indiana Jones unearthing, your sense of the sacred and mystical has been neglected for many years and is calling out to you to rediscover it. A damaged or desecrated temple symbolizes a hasty dismissal of spirituality at an earlier stage of your life.

If, on the other hand, the temple is a busy, thriving place filled with worshipers, you might be being called on to look into one of the more established religious paths for guidance.

DREAM TIP
Astral travel and déjà vu

Some believe that in your waking state, when you experience the sensation called déjà vu, it might be because in an earlier dream state you journeyed astrally and previewed the future. In your quest for an ideal partner, your spirit might find a soul mate on the astral plane. This person is sometimes referred to as a dream lover. The out-of-body phenomenon might explain concurrent dreams—the same dream experienced by different people in different places and time zones (see also *Out-of-Body Dreams*, page 115).

TOILETS

Dreams in which the humble toilet takes on an unusual degree of importance may represent feelings of extreme vulnerability, but just as often they indicate your body's suggestion that you might like to wake up and visit the real toilet sometime in the near future!

Where there is no real physical need, dreams involving toilets can symbolize the need to cleanse yourself of unwanted emotions or thoughts. The mind, like the body, needs a regular disposal of waste to remain healthy.

Dreaming that you are trying to locate a toilet in an unfamiliar place is usually an all-purpose anxiety dream. Where the dream ends happily, your confidence in overcoming niggling problems may be increasing.

■ FOR **TOTEM ANIMALS OR GUIDES**, SEE **ANIMALS** ON PAGES 28-29.

TOWERS

The significance of towers in your dreams depends largely on whether you are inside or outside them. Dreaming of being ensconced in a tower overlooking the surrounding world often indicates that you have a sense of personal achievement and security. Depending on the mood of the dream, however, a tower may feel like a place of imprisonment—think of the Tower of London for much of its history or the tower of Rapunzel in the fairy tale, for instance.

Since they feature so prominently in mythology and folktales, towers may be imbued with a magical quality, and may represent an attempt by the very powerful to occupy a space somewhere between earth and heaven. Being on the outside looking up at a tower in your dream may indicate that there is a major challenge in your life at the moment, an imposing structure to be infiltrated or conquered.

TOYS

A dream involving toys may suggest nostalgia for your childhood, or the need to reclaim aspects or attitudes of your life that you discarded in the years when being seen as grown-up seemed all-important. A dream of purchasing toys suggests that you are yearning for a simpler, more enjoyable life; dreaming of giving a child a toy indicates that there is something in your past that can be

of benefit to a younger person in your social circle.

Different toys have specific dream meanings, though these will always be modified by your recollection of the favorite playthings of your childhood.

ACTION FIGURES, TOY SOLDIERS, AND TOY WEAPONS

Real anger may be lurking underneath playful teasing or argument. If you are the one playing with such toys, an examination of deeper feelings is called for. If someone else is playing with them, you may be the target of disguised resentment.

BUILDING BLOCKS AND CONSTRUCTION KITS

Activity toys of this nature often represent plans that you don't feel confident about being able to realize. You may have scaled down your creativity a little too much. If you are particularly happy with something built with these toys in your dream, your subconscious could be giving you the go-ahead to get major projects moving.

DOLLS AND DOLLHOUSES

Dolls, particularly those in the form of babies and young children, indicate your desire for children but not for any of the responsibilities that come with them. Dollhouses may suggest that you feel a wistful longing for domesticity but are too involved with career matters to really focus on it.

STUFFED ANIMAL TOYS

Teddy bears and the like are usually the toys children take to bed with them and snuggle into for comfort. Dreaming of such a toy usually indicates a lack of emotional comfort in your life.

TRAFFIC JAMS

A dream that you are stuck in a traffic jam indicates that you are suffering obstacles in your path. Note in your dream journal, if you can remember, where you were supposed to be going. If you are stuck in morning rush hour traffic, the dream could be symbolic of the state of your work. You may be involved in a project where there are too many people and no one is communicating with each other.

If you are stuck in evening traffic, perhaps you are experiencing troubles at home. If the traffic in your dream has ground to a halt, you should expect to have to put some effort into untangling the problems. However, if you are successful in getting out of traffic, make a note of how you do it in your dream journal and apply a similar tactic in your waking life.

If you are watching traffic from a safe distance in your dream, you may need to seek help for a particular project that you have been trying to complete, but with no success.

TRAVEL

Transport and travel generally reflect imminent change and movement in your life and your attitude toward it. Dreaming of an unknown destination often indicates that you are unsure of the outcome of this change.

A dream about an adventure is difficult to interpret. You need to consider your daily life, then the dream's time frame, setting, and cast of characters. Such a dream might be a rerun of a past-life experience or simply the expression of a fantasy.

A leisurely journey is a sign of being in control of your life and its direction. The particular mode of transport may give hints about your current state of mind: air travel suggests quick, decisive action; sea travel, a need to have a very physical distance between you and your past; train travel, a desire for a firmly delineated path; and road travel, a desire for independence.

If you see yourself moving through a scenic landscape, you could be feeling a need to be on your own in order achieve growth in your ideas and awareness. Such a dream might occur when your life seems overcrowded.

A dream that you are walking suggests that you are about to have a breakthrough in understanding. This might relate to study or to the digestion of information. Aimless wandering, however, usually indicates that you feel exhausted and frustrated.

The direction in which you are traveling in your dream is also symbolic. Are you going in circles, up and down, right or left, forward or backward? Pay attention to the direction, and you will gain a new understanding of yourself.

TREASURE

A dream in which treasure is being sought may represent hope for a particular business venture, but if you have no concerns of that nature on your mind, it probably symbolizes a quest related to some other aspect of your life that you are worried about. Everyone's sense of values is different, but there are few people whose most treasured things are actually cold jewels and lifeless blocks of gold.

Dreaming that you unearth buried treasure suggests that the key to your values lies in your past; dreaming that you are burying treasure can indicate a fear of sharing your ideals with anyone else.

A dream in which you happen upon treasure in a familiar place indicates that the source of your happiness has been under your nose for quite some time, unnoticed and unappreciated. To find treasure in an exotic location, on the other hand, suggests that you need to travel to help you reassess your priorities.

■ FOR **TREES**, SEE **GARDENS**, PAGE 74.

TRILS

SEE ALSO **JUDGES**, PAGE 92.

A dream in which you find yourself on trial often suggests an uneasy conscience or a fear of being unjustly accused. The slightest and most insignificant misdemeanors or deceits of our childhoods can often lurk within our subconscious minds, gradually growing until some sort of imaginary mock trial seems the only way to

release this energy.

On the other hand, you may have some more substantial burden that you desire to be free of. A dream of being on trial, unpleasant as it may feel at the time, is often a healthy release of such internal unease. If the dream trial seems rigged, you might be experiencing feelings of injustice in your professional or emotional life.

TUNNELS

A tunnel is a place of darkness through which we must travel if we are to reach our desired destination. A short tunnel suggests that you are aware that this testing time is only temporary, but a dark, seemingly endless tunnel signifies a fear that you will remain far from the light for an indefinite period of time.

If a short, blocked tunnel appears in your dream, you may be unable to grasp a concept at the moment but nevertheless be approaching a solution to the problem. A cave-in in a tunnel suggests you are feeling claustrophobic, stifled by your career or living conditions.

A dream in which you are digging a tunnel indicates an overwhelming workload. Success seems possible, but a very long way off. A dream in which you emerge from a tunnel into the light of day is an extremely positive omen, suggesting that an ordeal has been successfully survived.

U

UMBRELLAS

SEE ALSO **RAIN**, PAGE 123.

This image is a signal from your subconscious that you should prepare for change or for extra or unusually heavy work. The umbrella represents security and protection—it is generally used to protect from either the rain or the glare of the sun. In dreams, rain is symbolic of emotional release, while the sun could represent the judgment of others watching your progress in a particular venture.

Dreaming of having an umbrella in the rain suggests that you can effectively protect yourself from the emotional problems or feelings of others. It could also indicate that you can be protected from your own negative thoughts, allowing you to get on with the job at hand. A dream about an umbrella may further suggest that you feel safe enough to engage in your own emotional release.

If you are using your umbrella to shade yourself from the sun, you will be successful at achieving your goals without interference. If you dream that you are carrying an open umbrella, you have finished your preparations and are ready for the next stage of your development or venture.

UMPIRES

Dreaming that you are an umpire or referee of a game may indicate that you feel a need to take control of a particular situation or venture to ensure its success. However, you must realize that in certain circumstances you will need to gather a good team around you to make the right changes. If you dream that you get into an argument or brawl during the umpiring of a game, you may suffer a family rift in your waking life; in that case, try to be diplomatic and see both sides of the argument.

UNDERWATER

SEE ALSO **DROWNING**, PAGE 57.

Being able to breathe underwater in a dream suggests that you have discovered that you are more capable than you thought, or that things have worked out more easily than you imagined they would.

Being immersed in water may also be an indication that you are facing a number of emotional issues. If you feel overwhelmed or frightened being underwater, make a note in your dream journal about the nature of that fear—you may be surprised at the emotions (other than fear of drowning) that appear. This dream may indicate that these emotions need to be resolved before you can move forward with your life.

If you do not remember the emotions of the dream, note your current feelings about drowning and leaving this life—what would you like to have resolved? Usually the first thing that comes to mind is the issue that your dream is seeking to reveal to you. Focus on this issue and make it a priority.

Dreaming that you are drowning, sinking under the water, is believed to be a warning that your finances may also be sinking and that your business ventures need attention, maybe some help.

If you dream that you are caught in an undertow, you may become caught in someone else's strong emotions— water is symbolic of the emotions—or you may soon be called on to comfort a friend in need.

UNDERWEAR

SEE **COLORS**, PAGE 44–47, IF YOUR UNDERWEAR WAS A
PARTICULAR COLOR; THIS WILL ADD TO YOUR UNDERSTANDING
OF SUCH A DREAM. SEE ALSO **CLOTHING**, PAGE 43.

If you see yourself in very unattractive
underwear in a dream, you probably feel
unhappy with your body image. You may
also be dealing with issues of
embarrassment, your exposure
compounding a feeling of vulnerability.
However, you can make changes to all
this—including your choice of
underwear in your dream—if you focus
on and resolve your feelings of being vulnerable.

If you are wearing very sexy and attractive underwear in your
dream, you probably feel sexy and attractive and find that life is
wonderful at present. Take care of your health so that you can
prolong these feelings.

UNDRESSING

Seeing someone undressing in your dream is usually a warning
that you should not share your confidences lightly at the moment.

The image of a person undressing is generally symbolic of
someone removing protection and revealing his or her true nature.
Interestingly, if the person undressing is the same sex as you,
this may indicate that you will learn of a secret or find information
that will explain something that has been puzzling you for a
long time.

If you are the one undressing, you may have formed a
relationship that may not be good for you, because the person
involved is not being his or her true self.

UNICORNS

The appearance of a unicorn, the symbol of purity and truth, in a dream represents a break from reality and the need to be less serious about life. It could be time to let your inner child out to play. However, if you dream of a dead unicorn, you may be facing a period of unhappiness and frustration where you are repressing yourself or feeling that you are being overly restricted by others. These restrictions may have arisen as a result of a lie or misinformation—check whether or not you really need to abide by or honor them.

Dreaming of a unicorn can also be a powerful suggestion from deep within your subconscious that you are in charge and nothing can go wrong. At such a time, you may feel very successful and notice that other people are aware of your achievements.

Traditionally, dreaming of a unicorn also indicates that you will be able to make changes much more easily at the moment, and that the changes you make will be of a long-term benefit to you.

DREAM FACT

Further teachings of Carl Jung

Carl Jung recommended paying close attention to the images we dream even though they may at first seem nonsensical or mysterious to our conscious mind. Jung taught that dream images were symbols, our way of giving form to something intrinsically complex and hard to grasp. This symbolic language comprises, simultaneously, both archetypal, universal meanings for these symbolic images and personal meanings determined by an individual dreamer's philosophical, religious, and moral beliefs. In his later years, Jung proposed that the deepest layers of the subconscious function independently of the laws of space, time, and causality, and are thus the source of such paranormal phenomena as clairvoyance and precognition.

V

VACATIONS

Dreaming of having a vacation is an indication that you will receive an unexpected present or sum of money. If you have not had a break for a substantial period of time, your dream of a vacation may be suggesting that you should rebalance your life and that you will rewarded in unexpected ways. Generally, vacations allow the practical side of you to rest. Once your mind is feeling more peaceful, your intuition can be heard more easily. Once you can hear your intuition, you will be able to see new opportunities and take advantage of them—relying on your gut reactions to guide you.

VALENTINES

SEE ALSO **LETTERS**, PAGE 98.

Traditionally, receiving a Valentine's Day card or present in your dream has a contrary meaning—you may be going through a period where you are not particularly happy with your lover or spouse, or a friend may be proving to be unfaithful or unreliable. This dream is symbolic of your hope for more attention from your lover or friend. If you are the one sending the Valentine's Day card or present, your efforts of goodwill and love will be rewarded, as you will meet a new person you can have a happy relationship with.

■ FOR **VAMPIRES**, SEE **MONSTERS**, PAGES 106-107.

VASES

If you dream of handling a vase that is empty, you may have to deal with problems and delays while your resources are low. If your vase is filled with water and flowers, you will triumph over the obstacles ahead of you without too much problem.

VICTORIES

Feeling victorious is often a subconscious stimulation of your conscious efforts to achieve a goal. Make a note in your dream journal about the nature of the victory in your dream. This may

indicate what projects are in need of further effort.

Feeling lucky in a dream usually indicates that you are on the brink of a new project, that important events in your life are imminent, or that you are going to meet some new people you will enjoy being involved with.

VIOLENCE

SEE ALSO **FIGHTING**, PAGE 67.

If you are the person acting violently in a dream, it is possible that you are feeling threatened in your real life, and are attempting to "eliminate" your competition in your dream. Your subconscious is allowing you to safely release your frustration and anger so that you are less likely to vent these emotions in the waking state.

Dreaming that you are being violently attacked traditionally has a contrary meaning—it suggests an improvement in your circumstances. Being the aggressor or witnessing a violent attack is believed to be an omen that you will become a lot more socially active with your friends.

VOLCANOES

Dreams of volcanoes are usually omens of some impending danger that must be averted as soon as possible. The rumbling of a volcano below the surface of the earth may be symbolic of the kind of danger that can result from a love being taken for granted, or it may warn against overlooking a detail, such as employing someone who is not really being reliable or failing to thoroughly check your security system, leaving yourself open to being exploited or burglarized.

WALKING

If something about your walk strikes you as unusual in your dream, try to identify the cause of your concern.

If you were walking with ease, your dream is suggesting that you will be able to accomplish your goal with ease. To find out what type of goal you may be going to achieve, look at where you were walking—a natural landscape signifies that your goal involves your personal development, a bank or store suggests investments or work.

If your dream surroundings are indeterminate, try to remember what you were wearing on your feet. Work shoes for business, running shoes for leisure, sandals for fun, or high-heeled shoes for romance and social engagements? If you were walking with some degree of difficulty, or the sidewalk seemed to be catching your feet, there are some obstacles in your path that need attention.

WALLPAPER

SEE ALSO **WALLS**, PAGE 156.

In dreams, wallpaper is associated with your appearance and position at social gatherings. If you have just freshly applied wallpaper in your dream, your social standing may be rising; cracks or tears in the wallpaper may suggest that you are the subject of gossip and speculation. Note in your dream journal whether or not you can remember any colored patterns in your wallpaper design (see also *Colors*, pages 44–47). If the patterns are angular and formal, you may be able to successfully build up your business using your social contacts. If the wallpaper pattern is curvy and informal, you may meet your next love at a social gathering.

WALLS

SEE ALSO **WALLPAPER**, PAGE 154.

Walls signify obstacles and restrictions. However, if they are load-bearing walls, these restrictions may be necessary—you must rethink your course of action. Generally, the load-bearing walls are those that support the building. They may also contain a door or a window (see also *Doors*, page 56, and *Windows*, page 160).

If you come across a wall in a garden or outdoor setting, you will have obstacles to negotiate. If you dream that you successfully climb over the wall or that you "magically" appear on the other side, your obstacles will be short-lived or easy to surmount.

WANDS

Dreaming of a wand is an indication that you may be asked to take a much more important role in a project or relationship in the near future. A wand has for centuries been a symbol of both power and the ability to draw power.

Note the materials your wand is made from. If the wand contains a gem at either or both ends, see *Precious and Semiprecious Gems*, page 121; if it is made of metal, see *Metals*, pages 104–105; if it is made of timber, see *Wood*, page 162.

If you dream that you are presented with a wand, you may soon be given a powerful present from an influential friend who has had a hand in your promotion or who will support you in your new role.

WAR

Dreams of war might be the subconscious's way of helping you release angry emotions—destroying an enemy or breaking through a barrier in your dream may represent moving beyond an obstacle you are facing in your waking life.

These dreams are frequently subconscious reenactments of the emotional battles in your life; if you have war wounds in your dreams, you may be finding it difficult to let go of the past. Note in your dream journal who you appeared to be fighting, where the fight occurred, and whether you won, lost, or came to an impasse. Your dream will give you clues as to what you are battling at the moment; you may also see ideas about how to resolve the battle.

Dreaming of the military aspects of war may also be symbolic of the battles you fight in your everyday life and business. Seeing an army marching in your dream usually signifies that you are defending yourself with increasing strength, either physically or verbally.

Traditionally, if a woman dreams of an approaching army, she must be careful with her safety and reputation. Other traditional dream associations include:

- watching a war—an omen of misfortune
- engaging in a war—a prophecy of illness
- men bearing arms—an omen of major change.

Dreaming of bombs and torpedoes symbolizes intense troubles ahead. The explosion of a bomb suggests that a long-term grievance is going to be aired publicly and will cause a lot of damage. If you feel that the anger is in fact emanating from you, look for more peaceful ways of releasing your anger, because a sudden outburst will cause enormous problems for you.

WATER

SEE ALSO **OCEANS**, PAGE 114, **SWIMMING**, PAGE 141, AND **UNDERWATER**, PAGE 150.

Water is a powerful element—it automatically takes the shape of any vessel it is placed in, flows easily around obstacles, and in time is capable of cutting through stone.

When you dream that you are in a pleasant, watery environment, you are probably being nurtured by life, feeling balanced and satisfied with your progress, and confident of fulfilling your potential. Calm and inviting water suggests the development of your imagination or a new stage in your life.

A dream of rough, turbulent water suggests that you are processing change, dealing with the associated uncertainties. Icy cold water might be a sign that you are feeling out of your depth. If the water is moving slowly toward unknown land, you are accepting new information. If it is moving quickly, there are changes you can't keep up with.

An image of water flowing over rocks or of a tributary flowing into a larger stream indicates that you are approaching a more tranquil stage of your life (see *Rivers*, page 126).

If you dream that you are being washed away by a mass of water, you may be unable to control your emotions. Being caught in a current suggests that you may need to find your own voice, rather than simply going in the direction that others are taking.

A dream in which you are unable to swim to land often symbolizes a fear of failure. A dream of drowning might be a warning from your subconscious that you have more work than you can handle and are falling too far behind to catch up without assistance. Alternatively, it may represent debts you fear you cannot pay.

WEATHER

SEE ALSO **ICE**, PAGE 84, **RAIN**, PAGE 123,
AND **SNOW**, PAGE 136.

Your hidden feelings are exposed in the climate of your dreams. If you dream of fair weather, you are probably feeling happy with life. Bright, sunny dreams are usually expressing your creative expansion and potential. They suggest that in relation to the subject you are dreaming about, you are in control and feeling comfortable and settled. Dreaming of a fair sky often means that opportunities are allowing you to do whatever you want to do.

Dark, gloomy weather in your dreams represents your fears and reservations, and the realm of the unknown. It may mean that you are unable to pinpoint exactly what is disturbing you about a person or situation.

Dreaming of cyclones, tornadoes, or hurricanes may be a sign that things are more complex than you imagined and you are in danger of losing control. If the weather in your dream is merely windy, opportunities for change may be coming your way, sweeping away past grievances.

Feeling cold or freezing in a dream suggests that your immediate surroundings are too cold—you may have kicked off your blanket! Traditionally, feeling the cold in your dream presages a fortunate change occurring in your life.

If you feel hot or stifled in your dream your room is probably too warm for you to sleep comfortably. Rarely, if ever, does heat have other symbolic messages in a dream—unless it also includes smoke or fire (see *Fire*, page 68). Traditionally, feeling too hot in a dream is a sign of the embarrassment you feel when you have to apologize to someone about your behavior.

WEDDINGS

SEE ALSO **MARRIAGES**, PAGE 102, AND **ENGAGEMENTS** ON PAGE 61.

Seeing yourself as a bride or being a wedding guest watching a couple get married is particularly lucky if the bride is smiling and the atmosphere of the wedding is joyful. Traditionally, dreaming of eating wedding cake is believed to be an omen of a long and happy marriage for yourself.

Ā dream in which the bride is crying—or you are aware that she feels she is marrying the wrong person—is a warning that you must be true to yourself now in order to avoid feeling trapped or publicly humiliated later on.

Dreaming about a bridegroom has curiously old-fashioned associations—delay in a personal or business venture; dreaming about a bridesmaid indicates that you may have delays in finding the right partner.

If the bride, bridegroom, bridesmaid, or wedding guests are wearing a predominant color, see *Colors*, pages 44–47.

- FOR **WEREWOLVES**, SEE **MONSTERS**, PAGES 106– 107.
- FOR **WHALES**, SEE **FISH AND OTHER SEA CREATURES**, PAGES 68–69.

WINDOWS

Dreaming of a building that has lots of windows or especially large windows usually indicates that you are happy with life, and open and communicative with people—everything seems to be going

right for you at present.

If you see a broken window, you may soon be looking for new accommodations; if you see an alcove or bay window, you may soon become more socially active and/or popular.

A dream in which you exit through a window suggests a release from restrictions or that you are inappropriately running away from your problems. An alternative interpretation is that you will be suffering from restrictions and obstacles but will find an unusual solution to your problems. Which meaning to adopt depends on how you are feeling in the dream—are you just glad to get out of the mess or are you feeling jubilant that things are resolved and you can go?

Opening a window traditionally indicates success in your ventures, and closing one suggests that you are going to escape a dangerous or awkward situation.

WINE

SEE ALSO **DRINKS**, PAGE 56.

Interpretation of dreams about drinking wine depends on what the wine tastes like and whether you are drinking from a bottle or a fine glass. If the wine tastes pleasant, you are entering a prosperous phase of your life and are now in a position to reap the rewards of your hard labor.

Sour or bitter wine suggests that there is something in your life that requires resolution soon. Drinking from a bottle indicates that you should possibly refrain from being overly social or that there are certain things you should be keeping secret. Dreaming that you are drinking your wine from a glass is indicative of good health and fortune.

WINGS

SEE ALSO **BIRDS**, PAGE 34, AND **FLYING**, PAGE 72.

The sound of fluttering wings traditionally indicates that you will be receiving good news from close friends or relatives. Hearing wings flapping violently is a warning that you may be gambling too much in terms of money or love.

Sprouting wings in your dream is a good omen, suggesting that high honors may well be yours in the future. If your wings are broken, however, your ambitions may still outstrip your skills—you may need to assess whether you should lower your aims or focus on acquiring more skills.

WOOD

SEE ALSO **GARDENS**, PAGE 74.

Objects made from a particular type of wood have
dream associations related to both the nature of the
object and the type of wood used in its construction.
The following are some traditional meanings of
different timbers:

- mahogany—luxury and inherited wealth
- oak—strength and longevity
- pine—contentment and happiness
- walnut—contentment and luck in love
- willow—sadness and hope.

WORK

SEE ALSO **OFFICES**, PAGE 115.

An image of yourself at work in a pleasant environment with
friendly colleagues suggests that you are happy with your workplace
and the people there. If the environment is gloomy, you may have
problems at work. If your coworkers are argumentative or if you are
the only worker present—the others being strangely absent from
your dream—you might be in conflict with your colleagues or
worried about losing your job. If others are able to enter the
workplace but you cannot, you might be planning to give notice
but don't know how to express your intentions.

Dreaming that you have an enormous
amount of work to do might be a warning
that you are using work as an excuse not
to look at other issues in your life. A
dream that you are contentedly
immersed in work might be an
expression of either your creativity
in reality or your subconscious
showing you the solution to a
problem that you have not been
able to solve in your waking state.

■ FOR **WRITING**, SEE **BOOKS**, PAGE 37.

ZIPPERS

An open zipper, especially if it is stuck, usually reflects a sense of premature exposure—you are not quite finished a project or task. A closed zipper often indicates that you are ready to perform in a work situation. A too short zipper may mean that you do not have enough material for a project. A zipper that is too long could be a sign that you have overestimated a situation; for example, you may not need as much money to complete a project as you thought you would.

ZODIAC SIGNS

Dreams of astrological symbols suggest the successful integration of other people into your life.

Strategies for Recalling Dreams

Dreams are the touchstones of a character.

—Henry David Thoreau

There are a number of strategies that will improve your ability to recall your dreams. Don't use the method below—or any other—unless you believe that your dreams can assist you in your life and contain messages you can use to lead you toward a happier, better life.

The first step is to train your mind. To do this, set aside a minimum of three to five nights a week for a period of three weeks to consciously train yourself to recall your dreams—let your mind know that you actually want to learn to recall your dreams. As a way of indicating your intention, try the simple meditation for remembering your dreams outlined on pages 14–15.

The second step is to set up your bedroom as a dream room, again indicating your intention to remember your dreams. It is important to set up your dream room as a place where the only thing you will do is sleep and dream. To do this, remove all the books, radios, and the television—and anything else that will distract you from your sleep—from the room. The electromagnetic energy field that is generated by radios and televisions is thought to interfere with sleep patterns, making it difficult to experience restful sleep.

For those of you who feel you can't go to sleep unless the television or radio is on, try to go without these stimulating images or sounds for a week; concentrate instead on doing some exercise in the evening to make your body tired before going to bed. Take a walk after your evening meal or play some games with your children or pets to help your mind disengage from your everyday worries or concerns—these might also be making it difficult for you to go to sleep.

The next step is to actually state your intention that you will sleep easily and restfully and that you will be able to remember your dreams when you wake in the morning feeling rested and full of energy—speak it aloud. Do this either when you have finished getting ready for going to bed or when you first lie down. If you're not comfortable with this, write your intention on a piece of paper and place the piece of paper under your pillow. Do this every night.

As part of your nightly preparations, place your dream journal (see pages 10–11) and a pen beside your bed so it will be easy for you to record your dreams as soon as you wake up. If it is dark when you usually wake up, make sure you also have access to some kind of light so that you can write down your dreams legibly without getting out of bed.

DREAM FACT

How your conscious mind works

The conscious mind, also called the intellect, or objective mind, is most active when we are awake. It is the part of the mind where we think, analyze and focus. It is said that our conscious mind is our perception or awareness at any one moment in time.

The conscious mind's major functions are thinking, judging, analyzing, doing and choosing. It is often referred to as the Administrator, Manager or Director. We can hold only a small amount of information in our conscious mind at any one time, so it is easy for the conscious mind to become overwhelmed.

Working with Your Dreams

Come to me in the silence of the night;
Come in the speaking silence of a dream.

—Christina Georgina Rossetti

Here are some questions to ask about your dreams. These are in addition to the basic questions on pages 10–11. Write down the answers to the following questions in your dream journal if they seem applicable to the interpretation of your particular dream:

1 Were you searching, playing, sad, running, alone, or in a crowd?
2 Were you a spectator or a participant, and did this role change in the course of the dream?
3 Were you male or female in the dream?
4 Were you young or old?
5 How were you dressed, and did this affect you?
6 Where did your dream take place?

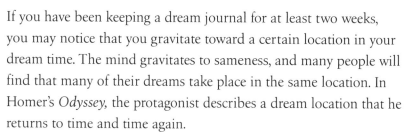

If you have been keeping a dream journal for at least two weeks, you may notice that you gravitate toward a certain location in your dream time. The mind gravitates to sameness, and many people will find that many of their dreams take place in the same location. In Homer's *Odyssey*, the protagonist describes a dream location that he returns to time and time again.

A landscape that recurs in your dreams will tell you things about your life—there may be aspects of the way you are living that you are not consciously aware of. When you remember your next familiar landscape dream, take particular note of whether the background landscape was full of vegetation and color and

---

DREAM TIP

Your subconscious mind's sense of humor

The subconscious mind has a sense of humor, and will often put puns and clues in your dreams. Be aware of visual puns when you are figuring out the meanings of your dream symbols.

abundant life, or dry and withered. Did you dream of mountains, oceans, a river, or a lake? Note in your dream journal what you saw and think about what these locales symbolize to you. If the background of your dream included a house, ask yourself what the house was made of. Was it a brick house or was it made out of wood, mud, or glass? And was there something unusual about its position—was it in a tree or a cave, for instance? Also note in your dream journal whether the house was old, new, in good order or falling down.

Here is a useful list of things to do with your dream journal.

1 Look at the whole story, no matter how disjointed it is, and see if there are any parallels in it with your current life and situation.
2 Read the list of symbols you have recorded, and make a conscious connection, asking yourself, "What do these symbols mean to me?" First take each symbol separately, then look at all of them collectively.
3 Imagine you are taking each symbol to your higher conscious mind, then allow your awareness to receive the insight of the message.

4 Record the symbols in your personal symbol dictionary (see pages 22–23), to compare their meanings here with their meanings in other dreams. This will help you find your common dream symbols.

Later in the day, or at the end of the week, compare and contrast your dreams, seeing what dream themes (see pages 168–169) each fits into. Patterns will soon become obvious. Considering all this will help you find your dream self, which is also symbolic of your waking-life self and the situations you are living in.

DREAM TIP

Controlling the location of your dream

Ask a crow totem to come to you in your dream so that you can get advice on location when you need a more suitable home.

Common Dream Themes

The glory and the freshness of a dream.

—William Wordsworth

Certain themes appear in most people's dreams. These themes relate to aspects of ourselves. We may never experience natural disasters in our lives, or take part in a truly significant and historic event, but when these experiences occur in our dreams they may parallel events in our waking lives. Here are some common themes:

Explanatory dreams

These kinds of dreams are about exploring your daily problems. While you are asleep, you receive all the information you need to resolve any life crisis in your wakened state. However, the dream is usually very abstract, and you may find it difficult to work out what it is trying to tell you because of the symbolism involved.

Nightmares

A nightmare is a vividly unpleasant, often violent dream that usually wakes the sleeping person. Nightmares usually stem from

an unresolved issue in your life, and tend to occur during or after periods of exceptional stress. Having a nightmare warns you that something you have repressed is affecting you—that the issues you have failed to confront are issues you need to deal with now. If they are not dealt with, they will recur, or become waking nightmares in your life. Generally, nightmares are not signs of sleep disorder or indications of physiological or psychological problems, but occasionally they do require treatment.

By contrast, night terrors—incidents of panicky arousal from non-REM (nondreaming) sleep—are considered sleep disorders. Night terrors occur more frequently in children, especially very young children, than in adults.

Recurrent dreams

The first type of recurrent dream is like replaying a videotape. An exact rerun might occur once a month, or once a year, rather than night after night. Its subject is an issue that you haven't resolved and might not have thought about for years until something triggers your subconscious.

For example, you might once have lost a key. This might generate a dream about a house without doors or windows (meaning you have no way to get into it), or some other dream that tells you to be more careful about small things. One day, years later, you might acquire a key similar to the one you lost. That night, and other nights too, the original house dream returns because subconsciously you still worry about the consequences of overlooking the small, but crucial, things in life.

The second type of recurrent dream is a theme or serial dream. For instance, you might have a series of dreams about traveling by bus to an unknown destination. This dream might recur about once a week. It might mean that in your daily life you are bored with your work but have not formulated any specific goals for resolving that issue. So in this dream you are constantly moving but you are ignorant of your destination. If you were to define your goals and establish a course of action to achieve them, this dream would cease.

Out-of-body dreams

Almost every person has at some point experienced the feeling that they have left their body during sleep, but many have not ever thought of it as astral projection. The astral plane is sometimes referred to as the fourth dimension, the dimension that bridges time and space. It is an invisible world of spirits, and the home of souls waiting to incarnate into physical existence. Out-of-body dreams are usually exceptionally realistic and vividly colored, but they seldom contain symbols and rarely need interpretation.

Past-life dreams

If you have a dream that is expansive, bright, vivid, realistic and yet feels out of context with your present life, or seems to belong to a different era, it might be that you are accessing your past, either earlier in this lifetime or in a previous life. A past-life recall dream might occur when you are attempting to discover and comprehend the meaning of your present life or are about to go through some change in your awareness. It might occur because you have a need to access data from the past to help you in these processes. Other triggers include meeting people you have known in a past life or starting to explore talents you have used in other lifetimes.

Dream Symbols and Archetypes

Dreams are the inexpressible that can only be expressed in terms of symbol or allegory.

—Carl Gustav Jung

Dream symbols can be objects, things, people, scenes, and colors from your life—unexpectedly simple or ordinary objects such as houses, people, modes of transportation, food, furniture, dishes, or mirrors.

They can represent emotions, feelings, health, work, money, and your beliefs about life. They come from your individual life experiences. As you think about your personal symbols, hidden meanings and truths from your unconscious mind will reveal themselves. The meanings of your dream symbols are personal to you.

Symbols may have a multitude of meanings, but a pattern will emerge in your dreams, making it easier for you to interpret them.

For example, dreaming frequently about ships on water may reveal to you the fact that you are always on a quest in life, but it may tell another of the need to move on and overcome obstacles.

Just as symbols personal to us and individual in their meanings appear in our dreams, so do archetypes—universal symbols. Carl Jung originated this concept, believing that archetypes are symbols that have emerged in the consciousness of humankind independent of our individual memories or levels of psychological development. They come from a universal unconscious, and are identical in all humans.

According to Jung, the archetypal unconscious is a universal memory bank that has been built up by the mental activity of humankind since the beginning of time. It is an inheritance we all carry in our unconscious minds.

ARCHETYPES IN OUR DREAMS

Archetypal figures and symbols are more prevalent in our dreams during times of crisis—they can serve as guideposts. Archetypal dreams often occur at pivotal points in our lives, and in times of upheaval. The dreams are often of spiritual journeys and pursuits, representing a search for some hidden aspect of ourselves. Having an archetypal dream will often leave us feeling that we have received wisdom from a source we do not recognize as ourselves.

Dream guides often appear in our dreams in the form of archetypal figures. Jung identified the following seven major archetypal figures that appear in our dreams.

1 Wise Old Person

A dream figure of this type could be a healer, doctor, priest, magician, mother, father, or any authority figure—often a dream guide we can converse with and get guidance from.

2 The Trickster

This is a clown or buffoon, a figure that mocks itself. It often interrupts or disrupts our dreams, exposes schemes, and spoils dream pleasure. According to Jung, it is a symbol of transformation.

3 The Persona

This figure represents the way we present ourselves to the world. It is the mask we wear in order to deal with our waking lives. When it appears in our dreams it often comes as a tramp or a scarecrow, a desolate landscape or a social outcast.

4 The Shadow

This archetype, recognized by Freud, is defined by Jung as the thing a person has no wish to be. It is the primitive, instinctive side of us. The Shadow reveals itself as a figure with mischievous, sometimes violent and brutal actions. It feeds on fear and hate, and persecutes others. Jung insisted that the Shadow is not evil, only primitive, and that it makes us aware of our darker energies and what we may be suppressing.

5 The Divine Child

This is the archetype of regenerative force, which allows us to realize our individualism. As the little child, it symbolizes our true self, the inner flame of who we were at birth and in childhood.

6 The Anima and the Animus

These are the feminine and masculine qualities of reactions, impulses and moods. This archetype serves as a soul guide, pointing us to the areas of our unacknowledged inner potential. The Anima (female) or the Animus (male) appears in dreams as a great person or as an animal of power, strength, and charisma.

7 The Great Mother

This archetype plays a vital role in the development of our minds, bodies and spirits. It is the symbolic great, powerful mother, and can appear in many forms—as a queen, a goddess, a female wizard, and more.

DREAM REPORT: ARCHETYPAL DREAM

"Betty" was on the verge of leaving her marriage, but she felt confused and guilty about wanting to leave a friendly, secure, and financially stable relationship. She felt depressed and in a rut, and this was causing her anxiety. Here is what Betty wrote in her dream journal:

I was at a party and people were all around me. I was alone, just watching everyone having a seemingly wonderful time. I was wishing I could just ask someone to tell me what to do with my life. As I stood beside a table full of hors d'oeuvres I noticed two people come into the room.

They were an older couple who appeared to be blind, yet they got around quite easily. They seemed to have knowledge of my concerns and understand them. Somehow I knew they were here to help me. I knew they had wisdom. I knew they had the answers.

The man came up to me and said, "What is it that you want?"

I said, "Will I ever find my love?"

The woman took my hands in hers and placed them in a big bowl full of dip, and pressed them together. She said, "Just ask from your heart."

I held my hands full with dip, and I firmly pulled them toward my heart, and as I did I simply floated up and up and up, and a voice said, "The answer is in your hands."

I woke up with my hands clasped to my chest. I felt clear and relieved, and I knew the answer at once. I knew I should be honest with my husband and leave the marriage. All my confusion vanished.

ARCHETYPAL DREAM ANALYSIS OF BETTY'S DREAM

Dream description: Party with blind people

Archetypal figures: Two wise people, outwardly blind but inwardly sighted

DREAM SYMBOL	CONSCIOUS SYMBOL	MESSAGE
Party, lots of people and activity	A lot going on, and things appear to be happy and active.	I'm there in body, but not happy, and I feel alone.
Wishing someone could tell me	I am seeking answers outside myself.	No one has the answers. I can keep looking, but no one but me will really understand.
Two blind people	People who can't outwardly see, but know and inwardly see and sense: they represent inner wisdom.	I have the answers within and I do know what to do.
Putting hands in dip	Something made by bringing two together (marriage). Hands in it means go and feel it.	Let myself feel what I have made with this person.
Pressing hands together	Joining, integrating.	Feelings need to be integrated.
Floating up	Ascension.	The need to rise above it all, move on.
Clasping hands to heart	Taking the self inward.	Knowing the truth in my heart.

Betty would now transfer the dream symbols to her personal symbol dictionary for future reference and comparison.

USING THE POWER OF DREAMS

Dreaming Creatively

*Dreams are true while they last,
and do we not live in dreams?*

—Alfred, Lord Tennyson

Once you have become skilled at remembering your dreams and interpreting them, you are ready for creative dreaming. Creative dreaming is the art of programming and controlling your dreams, and communicating with your dream self. Your dreams come either spontaneously or when you program yourself to dream. You can program or incubate your own dreams, and then interpret them. Creative dreaming gives you techniques for enhancing your dream time and going beyond the normal dream state.

All dreaming puts you in a trance state. This state has the same brain functionality as the sleep cycle. When you are in a sleep state or a trance, your focus is directed inward, and the impact of the external world is limited. Creative dreaming can induce the trance state for you. This type of dreaming can take place during normal dream time or during the day when you meditate, daydream, or take a nap.

Creative dreaming is the launching pad of dreaming. You can go beyond your "normal" dreams. You can choose to fly, to visit an old friend, to get answers to your problems, or to find peace and harmony. Follow the three-step procedure below to start your experimentation with creative dreaming:

1 As you descend into your dream time, take note of the images that come to you.
2 Drift deeper, with your eyes closed.
3 Allow the images to flow. If you are still conscious at this point, choose what dream you want to have—any type you wish.

As you learn to program and control your dreams through creative dreaming, your power to beneficially use your dreams will grow. You will be able to use all the tools of understanding and life enhancement that your dreams can give you.

You can consciously decide to dream on purpose, and train yourself to remember and interpret your dreams. Creative dreaming can enable you to use the following processes:

1 Dream incubation: You can program where you want to go and what you want to do, see, and find out about (see pages 176–177)
2 Lucid dreaming: You can have conscious dreams where you make decisions and control the dream (see pages 178–179)
3 Combined dream techniques: You can map out your dreams or deal with recurring dreams using an incubated lucid dream solution (see pages 180–181)

You can use any of these techniques deliberately in your dreams to explore, discover, recover, and search the infinite universe of knowledge. You can travel almost anywhere, and discover almost anything you can imagine. Consider going to one or more of the following destinations:

- **The Dream Library**—travel in your dreams to a "dream library," where you can do some research and get information on any topic. Search for books that you will write in the future or talk to people whose ideas you admire.
- **The Dream Doctor**—see the "dream doctor" to get advice, help with health issues, or information on how to maintain your health. Have a check-up with the best practitioners, get a physical tune-up, or have dream surgery.
- **The Dream Bank**—go to the "dream bank" to organize your finances or get financial advice.
- **The Dream Lovers' World**—visit the "dream lovers' world" to connect with your future lover, to discover ways to have a harmonious loving relationship, or to forgive and be forgiven.
- **The Dream School**—attend the "dream school" to be educated about anything you are interested in.

Also experiment with using dreams to strengthen your intuition and to increase the quality and number of prophetic dreams you have (see pages 182–183); meet your dream guide (see pages 184–185); or meet your future self (see pages 186–187).

Dream Incubation

My whole life
Has been a golden dream of love and friendship.
—John Dryden

Dream incubation is a form of creative dreaming. It was first practiced over 5000 years ago in Egypt, Greece and Rome. It is a way to deliberately induce a dream state. In the ancient days, the aspiring dreamer would spend the night in a sacred temple where people went for healing and guidance. The dreamer would pose a question or problem to the priests before retiring, and next morning the priests would interpret the meaning of any dreams the dreamer might have had during the night.

In our own age we can also program ourselves to dream, in a process referred to as creative incubation. This is where we ask for guidance, answers, or clarity on a particular theme. We can go within to our dreams for this. In all probability this will give us the guidance we need. With all inner dream work, intention, not ritual, is what matters. Follow the four steps below to help you incubate a dream:

1 In a positive and clear manner, state what you intend to find out or need help with (do not beat around the bush or have hidden agendas). Ask, "Should I change jobs?" or "How can I resolve this issue?"

2 Write down the question or request. Think about it during the day, and when you retire say your question or request out loud.

3 Before you go to sleep, remind yourself to remember your dream.

DREAM TIP

Guidance from animal spirit guides

Call upon a bear totem for strength, or, after making an important decision, an owl totem for confirmation of the wisdom of that decision.

---

4 When you wake up, record your dream. Be on the alert for any striking or unforeseen events in it that may relate to your question or request.

DREAM REPORT: INCUBATING A DREAM

I had been out of work for several months when I was suddenly offered two very good jobs. They had similar job descriptions: one was with a large firm, and the other with a medium-size to smaller company. I wanted to choose wisely, and was in some confusion about which job offer to accept.

I decided to use dream incubation to help me with my choice. The intention was to get clarity about which job to accept, and to remember the dream upon awakening.

That night I had an amazing dream. I was in a large factory, and many people were working, at an almost frantic pace, all around me. I was looking for the lunchroom, and no one would stop to tell me where it was. Suddenly I found myself in a small conference room.

Someone at the front was telling everyone about a new development. Before I knew it I was standing there as the instructor, and on my head was a crown. Everyone seemed to be listening and enjoying themselves.

I decided to take the position with the smaller firm. The key message I got from my dream was that I would get lost in the large company, but that the smaller one would allow me to shine.

DREAM JOURNAL EXTRACT

Feelings and emotions during dream: Confusion, frustration, curiosity, satisfaction, enjoyment.

DREAM SYMBOL	CONSCIOUS SYMBOL	MESSAGE
Large factory with many people, no one would stop to help	It's a big world, and life is going on all around it. People are. too busy to stop.	Lots of things going on and happening in my life, maybe larger isn't better.
Small conference room	A place to settle down and listen.	Realizing I can stop and listen to new directions in my life.
I was the leader or instructor, and people were listening and enjoying themselves	I was leading and instructing, and it was easy and great.	Go for the job that could offer managerial opportunities.

Lucid Dreaming

Our truest life is when we are in dreams awake.
—Henry David Thoreau

The Dutch physician William Van Eeden first coined the term "lucid dreaming" in 1913. Lucid dreams are those where you have conscious (thinking) awareness that you are dreaming, and you control the content and sometimes the sequence of the dreams. Some people levitate and fly in their lucid dreams. Having a lucid dream means:

- manipulating the dream state in the way you desire;
- steering the dream with a conscious reaction while you are dreaming;
- retaining awareness during the dream without awakening;
- having the chance, during the dream, to access all the memories and all the thought processes of your waking life;
- feeling the same as if you are awake—but knowing that you are asleep.

When we are dreaming, we become carried away in the dream and don't usually realize we are dreaming. Developing the ability to break through the dream state takes practice. Follow the three steps below to start experimenting with lucid dreaming:

1 Get into the habit of checking with yourself during the awake state. Ask, "Is this a dream?" If you do this regularly the habit will flow into the dream state, where you will also ask yourself, "Is this a dream?"

DREAM FACT

Knowing when you are dreaming

Carlos Castaneda, a Peru-born anthropologist, claimed that he had an old Yaqui Indian guru and guide named Don Juan Matus. Don Juan took Castaneda as his apprentice magician. Castaneda delved into dreams and the way to have lucid dreams. One method he used for recognizing if he was dreaming or not was to ask the question "Am I dreaming?" as he looked at his hand.

---

2 As you ask the question "Is this a dream?" look at your hand. If it looks normal, you are awake. If it looks disfigured or odd, you are probably in the dream state.

3 If you begin to feel yourself returning to the awake state, start to spin your dream self upward. This will normally take you back to the lucid dream state.

CONTROLLING YOUR LUCID DREAMS

When you are lucid dreaming, you can take control of the dream. Use the tips below to become a master of lucid dreaming. Remember that you cannot be physically hurt or killed in a dream. The dream is an altered reality, an illusionary world that merely symbolizes your real world.

In chase dreams, you can decide to turn around and confront whatever is chasing you. This is often the best solution. Whatever is chasing you will change as you confront it.

In disaster dreams, you can decide to control the upheaval and find opportunities for solutions. For example, if you dream of a tidal wave, with the giant wave about to pull you out to sea, you could imagine creating a giant boat that would let you ride the wave to safety. This would give you the opportunity to find a new land or place where you can be safe and happy, rather than a spot where you feel hopeless or utterly overwhelmed.

In dreams where archetypal figures appear, you can communicate with these figures—they are there to tell you something. If you wish to communicate, you will need to make a conscious decision to do so before you go to sleep. Dialogue with dream characters is easy: just ask them what they are trying to communicate to you. You could ask, "Why are you in my dream, and what you trying to tell me?" or "What is your positive intention about being in my dream?"

In dreams where you are naked and uncomfortable, you can ask yourself, "What do I need to know or change? And how do I make the alterations so I don't feel exposed or vulnerable?"

Combining Dream Techniques

In dreams begin responsibility.

—W. B. Yeats

Y ou can incubate a dream and then, when you are in your dream, control the dream to understand what it is trying to tell you. This is a particularly useful combination of techniques when you are dealing with recurring dreams or when you are using dream mapping.

You may find that you often consciously review things you are anxious about. This can lead to spontaneous dreams. When you have these dreams, you can use them to get clarity and assistance. You can also use them to start the process of dream mapping, which gives you much more control over your dreams. There are two ways that dream mapping can be used.

DREAM MAPPING

You can wait until you have a dream about a situation. Then:

1 remember the dream, write it down, and interpret the symbols;
2 decide to incubate a dream so that you can go back and have the experience the way you'd most like it to be;
3 remember the incubated dream and write it down;
4 translate the symbols, then determine the meaning of the dream.

Alternatively, you can start by incubating a dream—to be used when you are asleep, or for a meditation or daytime visualization— making the experience happen as you want it to.

1 Design the dream, visualizing yourself having the experience the way you want to have it.
2 Incubate the dream.
3 Remember the incubated dream when you have it and write it down in your dream journal.
4 Decipher the symbols and interpret the dream's meaning.

RECURRING DREAMS:
AN INCUBATED LUCID DREAM SOLUTION

To break the cycle of a recurring dream, you need to decide to seek out the dream's message and let it transform you. An example of this occurs in the movie *Groundhog Day*. Once the protagonist decided to make positive changes, he broke his recurring déjà vu dream, and there were positive outcomes and solutions.

If you have recurring dreams, tell yourself that you are going to find out what the dream is trying to tell you. Confront whatever is recurring or whatever the block seems to be. Recurring dreams only recur because they have not been successful in letting you know what it is that you need to understand.

DREAM REPORT: RECURRING DREAM

I'm in a school and I can't find my locker. Everything looks drab and the same, no one can tell me where my locker is. I keep going up and down the hallways, and up and down stairs. The more I look the more lost I get.

Incubated lucid dream solution: Step 1

My intention is to find the lost locker dream and receive any message it had to give me.

Incubated dream

I was in the school. It was a bit brighter and this time I had a locker number on a piece of paper. I was searching, and then I stopped in the middle of the hall and I asked, "What do I need to understand and do to find my locker?" I turned around, and the number on the paper and the locker behind me were the same—321. I opened the locker and it turned into a big room full of books, like a library. As I went

inside it was as though I had found a room where I could find solutions and answers. That was the last time I had that dream.

Premonition Dreams and Intuition

Out of a misty dream
Our path emerges for a while, then closes
Within a dream.

—Ernest Dowson

We sometimes have premonition dreams—dreams that predict future events. Often these require little effort to interpret. Some famous premonition dreamers include:

Abraham Lincoln, who dreamed of his own death. In his dream, so reports say, he was wandering around the White House following the sounds of "pitiful sobbing." Every room he went to looked familiar, but no one was there. He then entered a room to see a corpse laid out, its face covered, its body wrapped in funeral vestments. When he asked the mourners who was dead, he was told, "The President; he was killed by an assassin." A loud burst of grieving from the crowd awoke him from the dream. He told his wife about his dream. A few days later he was assassinated.

Elias Howe, who was perplexed by a detail as he worked on his invention, the modern sewing machine. He was not sure where to position the eye of the needle. Then he reportedly had a dream in which a tribe captured him and danced around him with upraised spears, threatening to kill him unless he finished his invention. He noticed something very odd about the spears: they had eye-shaped holes near their tips. Upon waking, Howe realized that this was the solution: he needed to put the eye of the needle near the tip.

Albert Einstein, who claimed that the theory of relativity came to him while he was in a twilight state of consciousness (sometimes referred to as a "power nap").

Robert Louis Stevenson, who in his book *Across the Plains*, related how entire stories would come to him in his dreams. He taught himself to remember and incubate his dreams. One of his dream-inspired creations was Dr. Jekyll and Mr. Hyde.

DEVELOPING INTUITION IN DREAMS

Here is a half-hour meditation to help develop dream intuition. Use it just before dream incubation or any other dream work. Record it so that you can play it back for yourself whenever you want to do the meditation. Use a watch to make sure the tape is silent for three minutes at a certain point. Read the following instructions slowly, with long pauses, then play it back to check that the words are clear and the reading is well paced.

1 Sit with your back straight and your feet on the ground, legs uncrossed.

2 Take several big, deep breaths and let your diaphragm expand as you feel yourself relaxing.

3 Hold your breath for a moment and then slowly exhale, letting all the air out. As you do this, let out all negative thoughts, all sense of limitation you may have been holding on to.

4 Now imagine there are holes in your feet, letting you take in great big breaths of air from the center of the earth. Let the earth's energy come up through your feet, to your legs, your hips, your trunk, your arms, shoulders, heart, throat, and head, all the way to the top of your head.

5 Let the breath linger there as you fill yourself with this earth energy—all that you need to connect and balance you.

6 Now imagine a tiny ball of light just above your head, your crown chakra, getting brighter and brighter.

7 Connect with this energy as you breathe it in. See it as a beautiful ball, spinning with all the colors of the rainbow.

8 This is the energy from the collective pure unconscious. All that there is to know, to learn, to be, is here now.

9 Let yourself be filled with energy, wisdom, guidance, and clarity. Connect with your intuition, allowing the two energies to meet somewhere in your body and connect to make you whole.

10 Bless these energies, this wholeness, and this power.

11 Let yourself float up—as a mind, not a body—to a place of peace, serenity and safety.

12 Now relax, and let yourself go higher and higher. Rest. Wait at least three minutes here before you continue. [Place the three-minute pause here].

13 Gently start to return down into your body, taking your time, down to the room. Hear the sounds around you, feel your body, and feel that you are fully integrated with your mind and body.

14 When you are ready, wiggle your toes and move your feet to help you feel the ground again.

Meeting Your Dream Guides

A thing of beauty is a joy for ever:
Its loveliness increases; it will never
Pass into nothingness; but still will keep
A bower quiet for us, and a sleep
Full of sweet dreams, and health, and quiet breathing.

—John Keats

A dream guide is a figure that appears to you in your dreams to give you an understanding of your life. It is something outside you, rather than your higher conscious mind, which you experience in your dreams as a sense of knowingness. The guide appears in human or perhaps animal form. Be open to what your dream guide may look like, and compare it with the seven archetypes that Jung described (see the list of archetypal figures on pages 171–172).

We all have dream guides. Some believe we have different dream guides for different situations in our lives. By programming yourself before you go into a dream state, and declaring that you will be aware of guides, you are opening the way for the appearance of your own guide. Continue to be open and patient, and you will not be disappointed.

Whenever guides reveal themselves to you in your dreams, attempt to communicate with them. If you should encounter any figure you feel bad around, ask it to identify itself. Trust your feelings. You can dismiss anything that does not serve you. Spirits on a lower plane can come in if you have not protected yourself against them. It is important to ask only for your true dream guides to come to you in your dreams. Dream guides cannot lie to you about their identity.

Make it a nightly ritual, before you go to bed, to say a prayer or protect yourself with light. This will enable you to have the best possible experience with your dream guides. Not only can you establish a rapport with your guides, you can also explore the dream world with their help and learn more about yourself.

MEETING YOUR DREAM GUIDE

Follow the six steps below to meet your dream guide.

1 Set your intention to have a guide appear in your dream.

2 Protect yourself with a gold, white, or pink light, to keep out lower spirits that may wish to bother you.

3 As you are getting comfortable and relaxing, let yourself imagine ascending to a place that brings you comfort and peace—a favorite mountain, the moon, the stars, or somewhere else you have not physically been to.

4 Record your dream when you awake, taking special note of any characters in your dream—people or animals, real or make believe.

5 If you communicated with these characters during the dream, what did you find out about them?

6 Invite your dream guides back to another dream session. Don't be surprised if, as you get to know them, they reveal their names and their connection to you. You may begin having a relationship with them—they will offer you guidance and wisdom.

DREAM REPORT: A DREAM GUIDE ENCOUNTER

I was walking alone through the forest. I knew I was looking for something or someone. Suddenly I saw a cave behind a waterfall. I was drawn to it, and found myself standing in the entrance. A big bird, like a hawk or eagle, came swooping in and landed on a rock ledge. As we looked at each other it was transformed into a person with a long white robe. I asked it who it was, and it said, "I am your dream guide."

Suddenly we were transported to another place, and the guide was pointing out to the ocean and telling me that my destiny lay over water. I moved to Australia, and now travel and teach all over the world.

This is the first of many occasions where I have used a dream guide to explore my life and find guidance.

Meeting Your Future Self in Dreams

Dreams are the facts from which we must proceed.

—Carl Gustav Jung

Sometimes we dream about the future. Are these "wishful thinking" dreams, or are they foretelling our future? They may not be premonitions, but they can show us what we are drawn to. Dreams about the future may help us understand:

- what is important to us;
- why we are spending energy on something that isn't worth it;
- what other path should we take in our lives.

DREAM REPORT: SEEING THE FUTURE

I had been worried about an illness that wouldn't go away. I had had several diagnoses, and tried many remedies. In a dream one night I decided to incubate a solution or (resolution) to it all.

I was having a dream about singing on a stage. It was as if I was observing myself—I was not really there. Then I realized I was looking at an older me. It was incredible. I knew this was an opportunity to ask myself some questions.

I remember the older me told me to keep on going, as the path I was focusing on was right. She said to enjoy work and stop living for tomorrow, as soon enough it would be here. I had to take life less seriously, and if I stopped trying to control everything my illness would go away.

I awoke to a feeling of wholeness, and knew the meeting had been real. I determined to take my own advice—and my illness left me.

EXPLORING THE FUTURE

What if it were possible for you to incubate a dream in which you could meet the future you and explore possible futures? Imagine going into your dream time to see how your life would be if you stayed on your current path. Imagine being able to get a glimpse of how your life would be if you changed anything in it. Try the following exercise—perhaps your future self, your older, wiser self, can become your ultimate guide.

1 Create a mental picture of the "you" you are now. Visualize this in as much detail you can, and with intense feeling. Once you have done this, leave the image for a moment.

2 Next, imagine going back five years and seeing how you looked in the past. Note the differences in your life, your environment, your behavior, your abilities, and your beliefs. Note how much you have changed, and possibly how far you have come, compared with that time. Leave this imprint there for a moment.

3 Now imagine yourself in the future, five years from now. Take note of what you'll be like if you continue on your current course at the same rate. Note how you feel about this future you. Leave that imprint there.

4 Now call forth your ideal future self, the one that has made modifications and changes and is the self you want to be. Don't think about how to do this, just imagine it. Then step into this "you" and let yourself experience how good it feels. Make an imprint of this future you.

5 Imagine you are still standing in the future. Look back at your present self, and ask the future "you" what is needed to take you to this future as fully as possible. Ask what you need to let go of or to change, and what you will need to start doing now in order to make the shifts you need.

6 When you return to the awake, conscious state, record your answers, and interpret your symbols. Have faith in the answers and follow the insights you have been given. You will be amazed at how well this exercise can work!

INDEX

Thunder Bay Press
An imprint of the Advantage Publishers Group
5880 Oberlin Drive, San Diego, CA 92121-4794
www.thunderbaybooks.com

All notations of errors or omissions should be addressed to Thunder Bay Press,
Editorial Department, at the above address. All other correspondence (author
inquiries, permissions) concerning the content of this book should be addressed
to Lansdowne Publishing, Level 1, 18 Argyle Street, The Rocks NSW 2000,
Australia.

ISBN 1-57145-994-4
Library of Congress Cataloging-in-Publication Data available on request.

Set in Birka and LT Ergo
Printed in Singapore by Tien Wah Press (Pte) Ltd
1 2 3 4 5   07 06 05 04 03